Christian Married Love

CHRISTIAN MARRIED LOVE

EDITED BY RAYMOND DENNEHY

IGNATIUS PRESS   SAN FRANCISCO

Cover design by Enrique J. Aguilar

Acknowledgments

The contributions by Malcolm Muggeridge, Fr. Hans Urs von Balthasar and Fr. Louis Bouyer were first delivered at the *Symposium on Humanae Vitae*, held at the University of San Francisco in July 1978 to commemorate the 10th anniversary of that encyclical's promulgation. Fr. von Balthasar's address was translated by Erasmo Leiva.

"A Summary of Karol Wojtyla's *Love and Responsibility*" was originally published in French, in numbers 39 and 40 of the *Fiches Documentaires de CLER (Centre de Liaison des Equipes de Recherche)*. The CLER is part of the French Family Life Bureau (*Pastorale Familiale Française*). It is engaged in the education, from a perspective that is fully human, of young people and couples concerning love and sexuality and particularly in matters pertaining to the regulation of birth and to marital problems. CLER is a founding member of International Family Life Promotion (IFLP).

"Eros and Agape" first appeared in *Revue Amour et Famille* (Jan.-Feb., 1971). This essay and Fr. de Lestapis' summary of *Love and Responsibility* were translated by Sr. Sergia Englund, O.C.D.

Contents

Introduction

The fact that the contributors to this book are either theologians or Catholic philosophers or, in the case of Mr.
Muggeridge, a journalist who is a "born again" Christian
deserves comment. Insofar as the birth control controversy
concerns the transmission of human life itself, it is too
fundamental a topic to be confined to theology or even to
religion. Anything that affects human life so profoundly as
the manner of controlling its transmission is bound to have
an equally profound effect on everything which depends on
there being human life in the first place: morals, society,
politics, science, art, philosophy, religion and, in fact, all of
civilization. Thus there can be no doubt that the birth
control controversy is a matter of concern for social scientists, secular philosophers, politicians and all who are committed to protecting and promoting human progress. I am
here, of course, speaking of the *rightfulness* of those whose
disciplines are formally outside the provinces of theology
and religion to investigate and pronounce on birth control
and related matters; the pronouncements of demographers
and social scientists as well as the policies of politicians and
nations, irrespective of their truthfulness or responsibility,
have already established the *fact* of their presence in the
controversy. But there is a fundamental sense in which the
controversy belongs primarily within the provinces of
theology and religion.

It is impossible to understand the significance which the Western world attaches to the human sex act apart from the context of the Judeo-Christian tradition. The dignity that this tradition sees in human sexuality has its explanation in the fact that it is regarded as the creaturely analogue of the creative power of God. Having made man and woman in his own image and likeness, he invites them to participate in his providence. In the sex act, they cooperate with him in the creation of a new human life. In doing so, they are also called upon to take responsibility for that life. Thus the sex act is a participation in God's fatherly concern for his creatures, as well as in his creative power, because parental love is at once protective and respectful of the child's freedom and integrity. Like God's love for man, then, parental love must risk rejection, misunderstanding and even ridicule. The lovers are vulnerable at the hands of both the beloved and the world. Yet, insofar as their sex act remains open to procreation, they freely accept this risk. But the willingness to accept risk is quite understandable in terms of the principle, "The good is diffusive". Just as God, who is supremely good, freely created the world in generosity and love for the creatures he would bring into existence, so the Judeo-Christian tradition views the sex act as an expression of love and generosity.

It is at this point that the Church's insistence on the impossibility of separating the unitive and procreative aspects of the sex act derives its intelligibility. For this is the act in which a man and a woman express their mutual love and in so doing donate themselves to each other in such a way as to procreate another human being. Because love is by its nature creative, the expression of their love for each other, which the act makes possible in a unique way, is inextricably tied to that act's openness to procreation. Thus, as Cahal Daly observes, to say that in marriage a man and a woman become two in one flesh is not simply to speak metaphorically; it is to state a literal truth as well. Their love is incarnated in the child. Even from a purely biological standpoint, the child gets twenty-three chromosomes from each parent. Thus, even though the child is a person and accordingly in his uniqueness is more than the sum of parental contributions, it is nevertheless true to say that in an important sense he gets his being from his parents. Since he is the embodiment of their love for each other and since this love is a donating of self, each to the other, we may fairly say that it is in him that they actually become two in one flesh. Indeed, as Daly further observes, this expression of their love will endure forever because the child is a person and, as such, is destined by God to live for eternity. This becoming "two in one flesh" is also verified on the dynamic level of day-to-day family relations. It is impossible to assess the husband's and wife's love for each other apart from their love for the child, while in turn their love for him cannot properly be assessed apart from their love for each other.

It is in the dogma of the Trinity, however, that we find the highest and most influential model for the sexual union between man and woman. Only in the Trinity is there love so perfect that the Lovers' communion—their respective donation of selves—is so perfect that the result is perfect unity, one God; and yet, because donation is an act that can be performed only by persons, their love preserves the uniqueness of the three persons, Father, Son and Holy Spirit. Because love is fruitful and because the love between the Father and the Son is a perfect love, it is the most perfectly fruitful of all love: its issue is the Holy Spirit. Thus modeled as it is after the holy Trinity, the conception of love between man and woman, as it has permeated the West and its institutions, is a love that is unitive without being destructive of the unique selfhood of each, and is also creative—it results in a new human person. And just as the love between the Father and the Son could not exist apart from the issue of the Holy Spirit, so the unitive and procreative aspects of human love cannot be separated. Indeed, just as the divine love is essentially and thus eternally trinitarian, so is the love among man, woman and offspring; for, as noted above, one cannot properly understand the love between man and woman apart from their love for their child and vice versa. In this mutual expression of a love that in its superabundance overflows to create a new person, both the man and the woman enjoy a self-fulfillment that they could not otherwise enjoy; for their growth in love for each other and their personal growth are uniquely dependent on the love and care they have for their child.

Now if the three attributes of the human sex act—unity, creativity, and self-fulfillment—owe their affirmation and emphasis to the doctrines of theology and the general cultural impact of religion, then the emergence of secularism threatens to erase them from modern man's perception of that act. For the widespread practice of birth control, along with the apologies for it, presuppose an entirely different model from the divine. The results, which are becoming increasingly evident, are marital disintegration, sterility and unhappiness.

The modern world is secular in that it is godless and thus stands in marked contrast to previous ages. But the meaning of secularism cannot fully be grasped except as a reaction against Christianity. There could never have been secularism if there had first been no Christianity. Hence, although "paganism" and "secularism" are frequently used interchangeably, they are not synonyms; "paganism" is, in fact, a misnomer when applied to the modern world. For the pagans acknowledged the existence of gods and of God, and it is no exaggeration to say that pagan culture was based on this acknowledgment. The Athenians, for example, attributed their legal code to divine origins, and when we read Plato's creation document, the *Timaeus*, what emerges very clearly is the conviction that not only was the universe created by God but that it remains under his providential surveillance. Secularism, on the contrary, rejects the existence of God and the transcendent, maintaining that human happiness and progress are to be attained by man's own efforts, if they are to be attained at all. The most spectacular example of this view is Marxism, which promises mankind paradise on earth through a rational organization of economic forces. But it is in the *Humanist Manifesto*, which first appeared in the 1930s, that one sees perhaps the most precise and explicit formulations of secularism's view of man and his relation to the rest of the universe. What the philosophy behind this manifesto comes down to is that not only is belief in God and personal immortality unnecessary for happiness and progress, it is antithetical to them.

How influential the forces of secularism have been in removing God and religion from the outlook of modern man can be illustrated by contrasting the latter with those of, say, Leibnitz and Newton. I choose these two figures because they were among the leading representatives of the then rising modern science. Although each understood the importance of mechanical and mathematical explanations of physical phenomena, they did not hesitate to refer to God and his power when they were convinced that a given planetary movement required his direct intervention for its explanation. Thus Newton found it necessary to rely explicitly on the sustaining power of God even in his theory of gravitation, and in reading Leibnitz's *Discourse on Metaphysics*, one is immediately struck by his frequent use of Scripture and theology in his philosophizing. Now it is true that these thinkers lived at the end of an era, at a time when the Christian view of the universe was crumbling and was being replaced by the secular view. It is also true that the impetus for secularism goes back before the rise of modern science. We must look, for example, to Latin Averroism, as it exerted its influence in the thirteenth, fourteenth and fifteenth centuries, for the eventual rupture between theology, on the one hand, and philosophy and the natural sciences, on the other. This rupture led to the modern belief that theology does not give us knowledge of reality; again, we must look to the Protestant Reformation for the emergence of the now prevalent view that religious belief ought not to influence science and politics because such belief is the result of "feeling" or "sentiment" rather than reasonable judgment. And although it would be a genetic fallacy to attempt to criticize Immanuel Kant's moral philosophy on the strength of historico-cultural influences, it would at the same time be naive to suppose that the dichotomy which he established between speculative and practical philosophy, i.e., between the evidentially justifiable claims of philosophy and the sciences, on the one hand, and the merely postulated claims of morality, on the other, did not draw its inspiration from the cultural forces initiated by the Reformers.

At all events, however, when we observe how stark the contrast is between thinkers even as late as the seventeenth and eighteenth centuries, such as Newton and Leibnitz, and contemporary thinkers, we get a sense of how successfully secularism has erased God from our scientific, sociopolitical and moral outlook. Whereas scientists and philosophers of past ages saw nothing out of place in discussing God and sacred doctrine in conjunction with their scientific and philosophical investigations, Christians of today infrequently give public witness to their religious beliefs or even speak of God in public. It is obvious that they are embarrassed to do so themselves or to hear others do so. The irony of it all is nothing less than Satanic. Modern man fears to speak of God, the Sovereign of the universe, but does not hesitate to speak out for the destruction of the unborn, for homosexuality and adultery. For example, very few readers of B. F. Skinner's book, *Beyond Freedom and Dignity*, or of Jonas Salk's book, *The Survival of the Wisest*, would pay any attention to the absence of God and religion in the views of man and the universe which these writers present. Yet it is from a deep concern for the survival of the human race that they write. The solutions they propose to the problems that now threaten mankind are, however, in their consequences dehumanizing; for neither Skinner nor Salk sees any value or dignity intrinsic to the human person apart from his contribution to the well-being and survival of the species. But in making such proposals, they are quite consistent with their secular, naturalistic starting point. Holding that man has evolved from lower forms of life and, in fact, that he is simply "mutated matter", they fail to see any essential difference between man and lower forms of existence. It follows that since matter in itself has no special dignity, nothing that is composed entirely from matter—not even something as sophisticated as man—can lay claim to special dignity. Thus the disturbing eugenic tone that characterizes Salk's writing at one point should come as no surprise, and neither should Skinner's rejection of any discoverable basis in man that can support claims of human freedom and transcendence over the social environment.

There are philosophical as well as theological reasons for rejecting secularism. The philosophical reasons cannot be entered into here, but then they need not be, for it is the right of theology and of religion to speak authoritatively on the issue of birth control that concerns us now. Suffice it to remark that, while the emergence of modern scientific method was not only a genuine advance for human knowledge in that it freed science from many traditional errors, some of which resulted from misapplications of philosophy and even theology, it was most unfortunate that this advance was accompanied by serious philosophical and theological errors, some of which were produced by misapplications of science. Because secularism rejects God, the Author of all being and life, its view of the universe, of man and of man's place in the universe is essentially distorted. This is certainly clear in the birth control controversy.

Consider, for example, the contrasting views of the significance of human sexuality as proposed respectively by secularism and Christianity. Secularism cannot help but appeal to naturalism in its estimate of sexuality. And naturalism, in turn, can hardly resist taking temporal priority for its standard of value. If we accept the position that man represents the highest ascent of life so far known and that life itself is no more than "mutated matter", it follows that the only standard for measuring human conduct is that found in the behavior of animals. It is not surprising, in other words, that the author of the now famous and allegedly pioneering work in human sexuality, *The Kinsey Report*, was a zoologist. And it is certainly not unknown that many of the self-proclaimed experts in human sexuality are either zoologists or physiologists or physicians and psychologists who subscribe to the tenets of naturalism. Man is only one part of nature, and if the other "animals" behave in a certain way, it is to them that he must look for his personal standards of behavior. There is, after all, nothing after man, that is, above him, but there is much below him and much which has come before him.

The fallacy here is that what comes first, what is prior in time, is the paradigm and standard of what comes after. Truly, plants and animals were on this planet before man and man is part of the physical world: he is bound by all the laws that bind protoplasm and he is driven by the same basic drives that dominate animal behavior—for sex, food and shelter. Nevertheless, man is more than a physical, biological being; he is a person, and to be such is to be a self, a unique center of conscious, autonomous and self-actualizing being. He is thus both physical and spiritual. As Thomas Aquinas observed, "man stands on the horizon between time and eternity." To be sure, this dual citizenship causes him problems. The extreme poles of gnosticism and naturalism testify to the difficulties that man has always experienced in trying to reconcile his spiritual self with his physical self. How much easier it is to identify man with his spiritual self and denounce the flesh as evil or to identify him with his flesh and reject his soul as an illusion. The truth, however, is that man is composed of spirit and flesh and that his spirit uplifts and transforms his body, so that he is a being of

matter who transcends matter. Although his so-called animal drives are in an important way the same as those of
the brutes, they are at the same time essentially different.
There are mere biological facts about the sexual nature and
activities of brute animals; the same cannot be said of human
beings. Just as eating is not for human beings simply an act
of physical nourishment but of social communion and
spiritual sharing (note expressions such as "Let us break
bread together"), so the human sex act is not to be ex-
plained solely, or even primarily, in terms of biology.

Owing to the fallacy of priority, secularism's conception
of communion—i.e., communication between persons—is
distorted and superficial. If we take the sex act of brute
animals as the standard for the human sex act, there is no
way of seeing that the latter is *sui generis*. Because the human
sex act is an act between persons, it necessarily represents a
higher form of communion than that which takes place in
the world of sub-human beings. The sex act of animals is
essentially impersonal because animals are not persons. It is
not an act in which one unique self freely gives, donates,
itself to another. Although it is true that, ironically, the sex
act of animals possesses an order and dignity that is lost to a
human sex act in which contraception is used—because the
former remains true to its generative function whereas the
latter does not—it is no less true that the sex act of animals is
infinitely lower in dignity than the human sex act that is
open to the possibility of procreation in virtue of the fact
that besides taking personal responsibility for each other,
the man and woman take personal responsibility for the
fruit of the act, their child. The ritual of naming the child is
a case in point. The care that characterizes the parents'

search for just the right name for their new child is but a sign of the child's preciousness in their eyes; after all, it is "their own" child with a uniqueness and value that only the parents can fully appreciate. And the name that they bestow on him or her is chosen with such care because it reflects the unique love and all the aspirations and hopes that they have for him.

I have said above that the child is the embodiment of the couple's love, and further that it is impossible to separate their love for each other from their love for the child and vice versa. But this is to say that the child completes not only the man and woman in each other, i.e., in their movement toward union, but in their respective genders as well. Because in being masculine and feminine respectively, each fulfills a lack in the other; as a couple, man and woman complement each other. This complementarity is not merely genital but physical, psychological, emotional, intellectual and spiritual as well. That is why relationships that are simply genital, that are based on sexual gratification, do not last very long: a simply genital relationship becomes quickly boring, and greater possibilities of sexual gratification with others become increasingly tempting. But if all this is so, then contraception repudiates the complementarity of the sexes and, in principle, repudiates masculinity and femininity themselves. The only thing that contraception can generate therefore is the androgynous society. Masculinity and femininity are, after all, unintelligible when the generative function of the sex act is denied. Not only is the love between man and woman that the act expresses impossible of fulfillment apart from the latter's generative function, neither is there any meaning to the difference in gender since the complementarity of masculinity and femininity is intrinsically bound up with procreation.

The dialectical movement from contraception to androgeny may be outlined thus. Contraception formally severs orgasm from procreation. This separation not only leaves the sex act sterile, it means that orgasm need not be confined to heterosexual relations and, in fact, not even to a human partner. The justification of contraception must at the same time be the justification of homosexuality and bestiality. For if orgasm can formally be separated from procreation, then, to put matters bluntly, any orifice will do and any instrument that produces orgasm will do. I am not suggesting that people who approve of contraception also approve of homosexuality and bestiality. My argument is that any argument in favor of contraception is in principle an argument for the latter forms of sexual activity. For of two things that are essentially alike, what applies to the one applies to the other. Seal off the penis or the vagina so that the sperm cannot fertilize the egg, and it becomes immediately evident that the vagina need not be the only orifice for sexual intercourse, nor the penis the only instrument.

It is therefore no surprise that, as the practice of contraception becomes increasingly widespread, the incidence of homosexuality should increase massively. The emergence of homosexuality as a socially vigorous phenomenon can be correctly evaluated only within the context of the contraceptive society. Homosexuality is, after all, the ultimate in sterile sexual acts that can be performed between two human beings. It carries to its logical conclusion the self-centered demand for personal gratification which characterizes contraception. Indeed, the disintegration of the family now in progress, involving, as it does, divorce, adultery, child abuse, abortion, pre-marital promiscuity and the subversion of the relationship between man and woman to rivalry and bitterness, not to leave out the aforesaid blatant homosexuality, has its source in the contraceptive mentality. For the latter challenges the intelligibility of heterosexuality, marriage and love. Although abortion, sterilization—especially involuntary sterilization —divorce and adultery are more serious issues than contraception, the latter is, in my judgment, the crucial issue underlying all these others. As long as the contraceptive mentality retains its hold on society, it will be difficult, if not impossible, to stem their tide.

In his novel *The Possessed* Dostoyevsky powerfully depicts the nihilism that godlessness inevitably brings in train. His character Kirillov proclaims that just because there is no God, he must kill himself. To the perplexed Pyotr Stepanovitch, he explains that, since God does not exist, then he, Kirillov, must be God, for if there is no Sovereign of the universe, then each person is his own sovereign. Since sovereignty implies absolute power, it follows that each person has absolute power over his own life. But Kirillov observes that there is one event in his own life—a crucial one at that—over which he had no control, his coming into existence. The only way left for him to assert his full sovereignty is to repudiate his coming into existence, and he can do this only by killing himself. He therefore blows his brains out.

The above scene displays Dostoyevsky's insight into the essential connection between theism and life and atheism and death. Man, who is a creature of God, is intrinsically insufficient in his very being. He has his being and fulfillment in God alone. By rejecting God, he cuts himself off from the source of his very being, and, like a beautiful rose cut from its root, soon withers and dies. Secularism is man's defiant proclamation to the universe of his self-sufficiency. But his self-sufficiency turns out to be no more than a self-delusion and his efforts to forge his own destiny turn to his own destruction. This drama enacts itself today; we see it unfolding on many levels, one of which is the widespread practice of birth control. God offers man life and death, exhorts him to choose life, and he chooses death.

Raymond Dennehy
University of San Francisco

MALCOLM MUGGERIDGE

Humanae Vitae:
What's Really at Stake?

I find myself in a most difficult position. After all, I am not
a Catholic. I do not have that great satisfaction that so many
Catholics enjoy. At the same time, I have a great love for
the Catholic Church, and I have had from the beginning a
feeling stronger than I can convey that this document
Humanae Vitae, which has been so savagely criticized,
sometimes by members of the Catholic Church, is of tremendous and fundamental importance, and that it will
stand in history as tremendously important. And I would
like to be able to express this profound admiration that I
have for it; this profound sense that it touches upon an issue
of the most fundamental importance and that it will be, in
history, something that will be pointed to both for its
dignity and for its perspicuity.

Of course I cannot hope to write the answer on this
particular subject because the answer has already been
delivered—two thousand years ago. In other words, this
matter which, as I have said, is of such tremendous importance, is an integral part of the revelation that came to the
world in the holy land, that stupendous drama which has
played such a fantastic role in the story of two thousand

years of Christendom: the birth, the life, the ministry, the death and the resurrection of Jesus Christ as recounted in the Gospels. This is the very truth before us today. And after all, that revelation, having been given to the world in those marvelous words of the fourth Gospel, that the Word that became flesh and dwelt among us, full of grace and truth; that Word, that revelation for all the centuries of our Western civilization, was itself carried by the apostle Paul to a Roman world which was as bored, as derelict, as spent, as our civilization often seems today. It was carried to it to animate it, to bring back the creativity which had been lost, to fill the world with the great expressions in music, in architecture, in literature, in every sort of way, of this great new revelation.

Now why do I think that this is veritably the foundation of my thoughts on *Humanae Vitae*? Because, in that revelation, an integral part of that revelation—also something that was wonderfully novel and fresh to a tired and jaded world—was the sacramental notion. So that out of, for instance, the simple need of man to eat and drink came the Blessed Sacrament. And similarly, out of the creativity in man, his animal creativity, came the sacrament of love— the sacrament of love which created the Christian notion of family, of the marriage which would last, which would be something stable and wonderful in our society, from which society it came, and which has endured through all those centuries until now when we find it under attack.

In my opinion, what has brought about this great weakening of the marvelous sacrament of reproduction, in the first case, has been precisely what *Humanae Vitae* attacks and disallows. The procedures whereby eroticism, instead of being justified by its purpose which is procreation, by its condition which is lasting love, becomes relegated to the status of a mere excitement in itself. And thereby are undermined not just relations between this man and that woman, but the whole shape and beauty and profundity of our Christian life.

Humanae Vitae recognized this and asked of Catholics what many of them were unable to accord, that they should *not* fall into this error, that they should eschew this dangerous procedure which was now being made available in terms at once infinitely simple, but also infinitely more dangerous; namely, the birth control pill. Now whether and to what extent this inhibition is or can or will be acceptable is not for me to say. What I want to say, as a non-Catholic, as an aspiring Christian, as someone who, as an old journalist, has watched this process of deterioration in our whole way of life—what I want to say is that in the encyclical the finger is pointed at what really matters. Namely, that through human procreation the great creativity of men and women comes into play, and that to interfere with this creativity, to seek to relate it merely to pleasure, is to go back into pre-Christian times and ultimately to destroy the civilization that Christianity has brought about. If there is one thing I feel *absolutely certain* about, it is that.

One thing that I know will appear in social histories in the future is that the dissolution of our way of life, our Christian way of life and all that it has meant to the world, relates directly to the matter that is raised in *Humanae Vitae*. The journalists, the media write and hold forth about the various elements in the crisis of the Western world today: about inflation, about overpopulation, about pending energy shortages, about detente, about hundreds of things. But they overlook what your church has not overlooked, this basic cause: the distortion and abuse of what should be the essential creativity of men and women, enriching their lives, as it has and does enrich people's lives—and when they are as old as I am, enriches them particularly beautifully, when they see as they depart from this world their grandchildren beginning the process of living which they are ending. There is no beauty, there is no joy, there is no compensation that anything could offer in the way of leisure, of so-called freedom from domestic duties, which could possibly compensate for a thousandth part of the joy that an old man feels when he sees this beautiful thing: life beginning again as his ends, in those children that have come into the world through his love and through a marriage which has lasted through fifty and more years. I assure you that what I say to you is true, and that when you are that age there is nothing that the world can offer in the way of success, in the way of adventure, in the way of honors, in the way of variety, in the way of so-called freedom, which could come within a thousandth part of measuring up to that wonderful sense of having been used as an instrument, not in the achievement of some stupid kind of personal erotic excitement, but in the realization of this wonderful thing—human procreation.

Now, of course, when *Humanae Vitae* was published to the world and was set upon by all the pundits of the media, it was attacked as being a failure to sympathize with the difficulties of young people getting married. That was the basis on which the attack was mounted. But, it was perfectly obvious, as was predicted some ten years ago on the BBC *Humanae Vitae* Symposium, that contraception was something that would just not stop with limiting families; that, in fact, it would lead inevitably, as night follows day, to abortion and then to euthanasia. And I remember that the panel jeered when I said particularly the last, euthanasia. But it was quite obvious that this would be so. If you once accepted the idea that erotic satisfaction was itself a justification, then you had to accept also the idea that if erotic satisfaction led to pregnancy, then the person concerned was entitled to have the pregnancy stopped. And, of course, we had these abortion bills that swept through the whole Western world. In England, we have already destroyed more babies than lives were lost in the First World War. Through virtually the whole Western world there now exists abortion on demand. The result has been an enormous increase in the misery and unhappiness of individual human beings and, most tragically, the enormous weakening of the Christian family.

Now we move on to the next stage in this dreadful story. And it is all this that is implicit in the encyclical we are talking about. If it is the case that the only consideration that arises is the physical well-being of individual people, then what conceivable justification is there for maintaining at great expense and difficulty the people who are mentally handicapped, the senile old. I myself have long ago moved into what I call the "N.T.B.R. belt". And the reason I call it that is because I read about a journalist who had managed to make his way into a hospital ward and had found that all the patients in the ward who were over sixty-five had "N.T.B.R." on their medical cards. And when he pressed them to tell him what these initials stood for, he was told "Not to be resuscitated".

Well, I've been in that belt now for some ten years, so I know that, as sure as I can possibly persuade you to believe, this is what is going to happen: governments will find it impossible to resist the temptation of the increasing practice of euthanasia, though it is not yet officially legal, except in certain circumstances I believe, for instance, in this state of California. The temptation will be to deliver themselves from this burden of looking after the sick and imbecile people or senile people by the simple expedient of killing them off. Now this, in fact, is what the Nazis did. And they did it not, as is commonly suggested, through slaughter camps and things like that, but by a perfectly coherent decree with perfectly clear conditions. And, in fact, it is true that the delay in creating public pressure for euthanasia has been due to the fact that it was one of the war crimes cited at Nuremburg. So, for the *Guinness Book of Records*, you can submit this: that it takes just about thirty years in our humane society to transform a war crime into an act of compassion. That is exactly what has happened.

So you see, the thought, the prayer, the awareness of reality behind *Humanae Vitae* has, alas, been amply borne out precisely by these things that have been happening. I feel that Western man has come to a sort of parting of the ways (and that as time goes on you who are much younger will realize this). These two ways of looking at our human society will be side by side, and it will be necessary to choose one or the other. On the one hand, the view of mankind which has all through the centuries of Christendom been accepted in one form or another by Western people: that we are a family; that mankind is a family with God who is the father. In a family you don't throw out the specimens that are not up to scratch. In a family you recognize that some will be intelligent and some will be stupid, some will be beautiful and some will be ugly. But what unites the family is the fatherhood of God. On the other hand, our way of life is now moving towards the replacement of this image of the family by the image of a factory farm in which what matters is the economic prosperity of the family and of the livestock, so that all other considerations cease to be relevant. And you will find that this terrible notion increasingly occupies the minds of people and becomes acceptable to them.

There is something else that is envisaged in the encyclical that we are talking about. Mother Teresa's work—and to me this has been one of the great illuminations of life—her work itself is a sort of confutation of all the calculations behind this humanistic, scientific view of the world, of life which the media and other influences are foisting upon our Western people. She considers it worthwhile to go to infinite trouble to bring a dying man in from the street in order that perhaps only for five minutes he may see a loving Christian face before he finally dies. A procedure which, in scientific terms or humanistic terms, is completely crazy, but which I think increases enormously the beauty and the worthwhileness of being a human being in this world.

Similarly with children. She boasts—and the boast is true I can assure you—that their children's clinic has never under any circumstances refused, however crowded it might be, to take in a child who wants to come there. I don't know if you saw the television program that was made about her called "Something Beautiful for God", but in it, there is one episode that always sticks in my mind. And that is when I was walking up the steps with her and there was a little baby that had just been brought in, so small that it seemed almost inconceivable that it could live. And I say rather fatuously to Mother Teresa, "When there are so many babies in Calcutta and in Bengal and in India, and so little to give them, is it *really* worthwhile going to all this trouble to save this little midget?" And she picks up the baby and she holds it, and she says to me, "Look! There's life in it." Now that picture is exactly what *Humanae Vitae* is about.

I could write until kingdom come about it and it would not give such a clear notion as just that episode does. "Look! There's life in it." And life comes from God. Life, any life, contains in itself the potentialities of all life, and therefore deserves our infinite respect, our infinite love, our infinite care. All ideas that we can get rid of manifestations of life which may be inconvenient or burdensome to us, that we can eliminate from our carnal appetites the consequences of carnality in terms of new life; all these notions are of the devil. They all come from below. They are all from the worst that is in us. The triumphant words, "There's life in it", this is what we Christians have got to think about and hold on to in times when all that this signifies is and will be under attack.

I do not wish to close leaving the impression with you that I feel pessimistic. Of course, I can see, as anyone must who looks at what is going on in the world, the terrible dangers. Pascal puts it very well, you know. He says that when men try to live without God—which is what, in fact, is happening in the Western world now, men and women are trying to live without God—Pascal says when they do that, there are two inevitable consequences: either they suppose that they are gods themselves and go mad (and we have seen enough of that in our time), or they relapse into mere animality. And of course, what Pascal himself did not see is that even to say they relapse into animality is a kind of gloss on what truly happens. It is something much worse than animality. It is not losing the sacramental ideal of carnality, of eating, in order to have the mere animal idea, rather it is moving from the sacramental notion to the really sick notion of treating something that is by its nature related to this human creativity as itself a pleasure, and a pleasure that we should demand to have.

Now I do not want you to think that in pointing that out I am merely indulging in pessimism. Because it is not so. It is not possible to love Christ and to love the Christian faith and to see what it has done for Western man in the last two thousand years without feeling full of hope and joy. Of course it is possible that the particular civilization that we belong to can collapse, as others have. Of course it is possible that what is called Christendom can come to an end. But Christ cannot come to an end. And when we look round, even in this somber world of today, we have to notice one enormously hopeful thing. And that is, that the efforts to create this world without God—whether through the means of shaping men and controlling men and molding men into a particular sort of human being, as the Communists have sought to do, or by merely accepting libertinism, or self-indulgence, as Western people have sought to do—have, in both cases, proved a colossal failure. From Communist countries we have had the voice of someone like Solzhenitsyn. In his recent speech at Harvard, which was a marvelous speech, he said that out of the great suffering of the Russian people would come some new great hope and understanding that the world lacked. And that out of the very failure of our efforts in the West to escape from the reality of God by the absurdities of affluence, we might expect men to recover their sense of what is real and to escape from a world of fantasy.

You know, it is a funny thing. When you are old there is something that happens that I find very delightful. You often wake up about half-past two or three in the morning when the world is very quiet and, in a way, very beautiful. And you feel half-in and half-out of your body. As though it is really a toss-up whether you go back into that battered old carcass that you can actually *see* between the sheets, or make off to where you see in the sky, as it were, like the glow of a distant city, what I can only describe as Augustine's City of God. It is a strange thing, but you are aware of these two things: of the old battered carcass and your life in it and this wonderful making-off. And at that moment, in that sort of limbo between those two things, you have an extraordinarily clear perception of life and everything. And what you realize with a certainty and a sharpness that I cannot convey to you is, first of all, how extraordinarily beautiful the world is; how wonderful is the privilege of being allowed to live in it, as part of this human experience; of how beautiful the shapes and sounds and colors of the world are; of how beautiful is human love and human work, and all the joys of being a man or a woman in the world. And at the same time, a certainty past any word that I could pass to you, that as a man, a creature, an infinitesimal part of God's creation, you participate in God's purposes for his creation. Whatever may happen, whatever men may do or not do, whatever crazy projects they may lend themselves to, those purposes of God are loving and not hating, creative and not destructive, universal and not particular, and in that awareness one finds great comfort and great joy.

Certainly, *Humanae Vitae* bears witness to the beauty of God's creation and provides the foundation for hope in life. With this same certainty, we must be thankful that God's purpose for human life shines through with such clear splendor in the teaching of this document.

LOUIS BOUYER

The Ethics of Marriage:
Beyond Casuistry

There are a number of people who suppose that it is the publication of *Humanae Vitae* that has caused the retreat from Catholic practice and belief of so many men and women during the last ten years. Without neglecting the natural disappointment experienced by a number of people who had been lulled by the hope that the traditional Christian requirements in that field could be relaxed, it must be said that that explanation, although it has been accepted even by some famous sociologists, is a conspicuous example of the policy expressed in the saying, *"post hoc ergo propter hoc"*. That is, in this case as in many others, the fact that something has happened after some other thing does not necessarily mean that the second thing has been caused by the first. Indeed, already before *Humanae Vitae*, the crisis which immediately followed the Council had begun to develop. It was that crisis in belief and practice which had already provoked the defection of so many people. And, be it observed, no less, perhaps, of people scandalized by a new laxity admitted and even proclaimed by supposedly Catholic priests, theologians, religious of both sexes, than of people who abandoned their former

Christian behavior together with what had been their faith until then. And if something has undoubtedly developed and emphasized the double process of de-Christianization after *Humanae Vitae*, it is certainly much more the incredible lack of a positive response it has encountered on the part of so many Catholic leaders than the demands it made upon the fidelity and generosity of the average Catholic layman and laywoman.

At the time when the encyclical appeared, I was myself teaching in what was then still one of the main seats of Catholic learning in the United States. Incredible propaganda was immediately launched there by some would-be theologians against the Pope and his teaching before anybody had read or even seen the document, only because it was rumored that it did not just drop what had been considered since the very beginning of Christianity as the Christian vision of contraception.

Certainly, there were quite a few people who felt disheartened by the fact they were not given what most foolish-thinking, self-appointed reformers had led them to expect. But there were clearly many more who felt disgusted with the Church, where teachers in an official position, priests and religious, could not only count for nothing what they had until then acknowledged as the supreme authority, but not even take the trouble to ascertain exactly what the authority was teaching before rejecting it.

More generally speaking, the fundamental factor which explains the disappointment felt by so many Catholics already before *Humanae Vitae* but still more since it appeared, and their subsequent defection, is the incredible anarchy which has developed in the last fifteen years or so, first among the religious who should be the examples of fidelity to Christ and the Church, then, among the clergy in general, and especially those having a special responsiblity for teaching the Catholic truth.

However, if *Humanae Vitae* has provided only a major test of the most sudden decomposition of the Catholic spirit among so many of those who should have been its main supporters, it was soon all the more remarkable to see how many non-Catholics and even non-Christians—doctors, moralists, social thinkers—openly declared that the Pope had taken a position urgently needed in a period when sexuality tended to be considered, especially through the impact of the mass media, as totally divorced from any ethical considerations. More precisely, the most perceptive of these observers, in an ever-growing number through the last years, have come to declare that the Pope had been the first to try to oppose seriously a growing contempt for the sacredness of life which could prove soon to be the self-inflicted death blow of our permissive society.

It is evident now for all those, Catholic or not, Christian or not, who still have eyes to see, that *Humanae Vitae*, whatever may have been its possible defects, was, first and most, a needed attempt to resist the fatal tendency towards the complete disintegration, not only of the Christian, but of any kind of humanistic morality based upon respect for human life as such.

A second point to be underlined is that *Humanae Vitae* has done that, not by teaching anything new, but just by maintaining that it was no more in the power of the Pope than of any other teacher to teach, on the point considered now, something else than what has been taught from the beginning of Christianity and what had come to be accepted by the best minds of mankind under the Christian influence: that the life of man, and even of the most frail human being, such as one just coming to birth, was sacred and could not be sacrificed to any egotistical or even collective convenience.

At the time when the encyclical appeared, it was proclaimed by all kinds of propaganda that wider and freer use of contraceptives was the only way to repress the development of abortion. However, since that time, it has been discovered that the development of a complete freedom in the use of contraception, far from eliminating abortion, is leading towards a similar plea for the total freedom of abortion.

And now, it is clear that after abortion has become lawful in so many countries, we are going to legalize euthanasia. And what next after euthanasia? Freedom to suppress all the possible misfits? All those considered as obstacles to an easier way of life for the majority? So true it is that to have respect for life is something which cannot be divided. It is either an absolute not to be tampered with or it is doomed to disappear altogether, and much more quickly than even the most pessimistic observers could have thought possible a few years ago.

This should be enough to make us realize that a constant teaching of the Church for two thousand years, based upon the teaching of the whole Bible and grounded upon the deepest instinct of human nature, cannot be altered or simply disregarded without immediately having the most baleful effects instead of the expected liberation. When all that has been fully realized, we have not, for all that, to suppose that *Humanae Vitae* by itself has said or done everything which had to be said or done on the matter.

Humanae Vitae limited itself to giving an answer to a question as that question had been posed: Can we now drop the barrier which had been opposed through centuries to the disintegration of sexual ethics for a higher possibility of enjoyment or convenience desired by many men and women of today? The answer was "no". And it could not be other than "no". But, just as the problem could not be reduced to the question as it had been posed, it cannot be solved by the unavoidable answer given to it. *Humanae Vitae* gave a casuistic answer to a casuistic question. But the very trouble it has occasioned is a sign that Christian ethics cannot be reduced to a casuistical of protection around Christian morality proper. They cannot provide for its basis and justification. And we must say it openly: it is not even just a matter here of a positive morality, one which goes beyond the merely negative. It is a problem of the development of what is most essential in Christian spirituality, the true nature and implications of love worthy of the name, which goes far beyond even the most positive constructive vision of the moral law.

Our first object in this paper, then, will be to develop and try to make as clear as possible these two points. First, it is certain that we cannot dispense with casuistry, for there will ever be questions posed about whether this or that may be done or not, and these questions cannot be evaded. However, it is the death of true ethics when it tends to be reduced to casuistry. For then ethics becomes just a collection of prohibitions, when it should show the right way to live and to lead a fully human life. But when casuistry occupies or seems to occupy all the ground of moral thinking, then it is unavoidable that ethics appears to be the opposite of what it should be; it will appear as a way of limiting, restricting human life, an obstacle to its free development and finally, the imposition upon natural aspirations of most unnatural constraints.

Now, where this has become the impression ethics gives, we must say that morality, if not dead, certainly is dying. For morality as such is obedience to the very law of our nature. That is to say, not an unnatural or anti-natural crushing of our being, but its own way of fruitful development. Such an obedience to such a law, therefore, far from implying any artificial constraint, is the only possible form of self-realization in which freedom will appear as creative and constructive, and not destructive.

However, this cannot be if there is not a positive goal presented to moral endeavor which will justify any ethical prohibition as a necessary protection of our effective progress towards that goal. To come immediately to the problem: all the prohibitions connected with human sexuality cannot make sense as long as they are not seen as so many safeguards of life, of human life, of its full and fully human growth. In other words, we are to see how it is through love, love which is fulfillment of ourselves as well as of our loved ones and fulfillment of the couple themselves in the common creativity of their union—it is *that* which imperatively implies a renunciation of whatever could prove a check, an obstacle, an obstruction, to that harmonious and healthy realization of a man and woman.

To say this, to see everything in the light of this, is needed to justify the demands made upon us by any sexual ethics so as to make them acceptable. However, when we are here we have to be clear, much clearer than men generally are today, about what we mean by "love", and especially sexual love. Certainly, in more or less current presentations of sexual morality in the last century, there was a tendency to focus everything upon what was called "the primary end" of marriage, especially of sexual union, that is to say, the procreation of children. It was a well-meant reaction which brought back to light what was a positive value and what was called "the secondary end" of marriage, that is, the mutual happiness and fulfillment of husband and wife in their union.

Nonetheless, we must insist immediately that that very distinction between the primary end and the secondary end of married life and sexuality could easily become and has proved to have become a most ambiguous solution of the possible difficulties. For these two ends of marriage not only are not separable but cannot even be adequately distinguished. Just, indeed, as in true love, the happiness and self-realization of husband or wife cannot be separated, nor even neatly distinguished from that of the other spouse, neither can it be done with their mutual happiness or mutual fulfillment in their procreation—and we would add immediately, the education—of children. This, in fact, is not something external to their mutual love, to the community of life which is that of husband and wife together. It is not even conjoined to it. It is an integral part of it, of its normal development, of its actual fulfillment. To realize this, we must see first that love, human sexual love, if it is authentic, is of course something more than sensual satisfaction, even if it certainly includes it. But it is no less important to see that it is not only something more, but definitely something else than what has come to be understood as romantic love. Not only is it more than any sentimental self-complacency in reciprocal enjoyment of one by the other, it goes beyond mutual fulfillment of each in and through the other. It must be said that it implies something entirely different from that. More exactly, it is the very nature of sexual love as such to imply that one who loves does not love just so as to become fully oneself, even if it is understood that one's own self-fulfillment implies that of the other. It is of the very essence of sexual love as such to imply and to urge a not only mutual, but common opening of the two beings coming to union. It involves their common orientation towards what transcends the two as well as each of them; what will make each and both together discover that they can be fully themselves, only, as it were, beyond themselves, in a common interest, where both are to be lost, and more precisely, in a common creativity where their own being as well as their mutual love will find a plenitude of realization which could no more be found in their mere encounter than in the solitude of each.

That does not mean of course that in every thought, feeling, action which joins one with the other, the thought of and preoccupation with the children to come or who are already there, is to be fully actual and explicit. But it means certainly that not only can there not be an exclusion without negating to the core the very mutual reciprocal correlation between the two spouses, but that the thought of and preoccupation with those to be the product of the life of the couple as such is necessarily latent in the whole of their union and intimacy.

To put it concretely, in a very plain sentence of the French writer, Saint-Exupery, "True love does not so much consist of looking perpetually into one another's eyes as of looking together to the same goal." And we may add immediately that that necessary goal is not just a physical procreation, not even the total education of children, but normally, in and through that, a universal orientation of all the life of the couple towards human creativity in the widest and deepest possible sense.

There is a very simple test of the truth of what I have just said: It has been observed often that the couples which may seem at first most entirely absorbed in their mutual love, so much that they do not even see the necessary relation there should be between mutual love and creative love, sooner or later (and usually sooner than later) turn to mutual destruction.

Their union, or what seemed to be such, being not founded upon mutual surrender and mutual generosity, is quickly revealed in its true nature as not union–communion but an unhealthy tendency to absorb, as it were, the one into the other. These apparently sublime conjunctions of romantic souls, each one apparently lost in the other, reveal themselves to be like those copulations of some insects which end regularly in one devouring the other in and through their conjunction. Even when it is not so, it is a fact of common observation that no normal human couple can survive easily in their mutual love if they are unable to procreate, except if they agree then to adopt children or at least to devote themselves together to some creative activity which will turn them together outside their self-enclosed society.

Let us remark that until now we have based all our developments upon a pure analysis of human nature, of human sexuality considered only in its physical, psychological and sociological implications. But it must be clear already that we cannot do that without opening the way to the higher considerations of Christian theology and spirituality. For the Christian, the supernatural vocation of man is not just something super-added to his nature. It is something for which that nature was intended from the first by its creator. It was prepared for it; preadapted to it. And it is true, reciprocally, that our human nature cannot understand itself fully until, by a free relation and communication of God, it has grown to a realization of what it could not reach or even imagine or even conceive without that supernatural gift. This will bring us to what is properly the Christian view of marriage, and the Christian possibilities of fulfilling it adequately.

It is very remarkable first of all that the Old Testament already made very clear the paradox involved in sexuality as it was willed when God created man. On the one hand, in opposition to all the fertility cults of Canaan and the Near East in general, with their multiple mother goddesses, their sacred prostitutions and all their orgiastic kinds of worship, the biblical revelation made it absolutely clear that God in himself, in his eternal transcendent life, has nothing to do with sexuality. As it will be expressed by the greatest Christian thinker of the fourth century, Gregory of Nyssa, precisely because God is the source of life, has and is life in its fullness, he is a virginal being par excellence.

However, the same prophets who were the most eager to maintain that vision of God against all the relapses of Israel in idolatry were also the first to maintain the sacredness of sexuality, although in a completely different perspective from that of contemporary paganism. First, for them, life—the blood which is, as it were, its medium—is sacred because it is a manifestation of what God is in himself and intends to be for his creatures. When it has been realized that this is the basis for all their thinking, we understand that all the sexual taboos of the Old Testament, far from implying any contempt of sexuality meant that just because it is so closely connected with the blossoming and fructifying of life, it is a field of a most mysterious encounter of man with God, where man must ever remember that he is not free to make of it what he wills as the sinner, but what God wills as the holy one.

However, at the same time as it was discovered by Israel that the holiness of God is that of the only true and perfect love, the same prophets, beginning with Hosea and followed by Jeremiah and Ezekiel, were to teach that the differentiation between the two sexes and their conjunction, if it had no counterpart in the transcendent being, in the life of God, was to be seen as the basic expression of his intended relationship with his creature and, above all, with humanity. In so far as his eternal love has become manifested in time by all creation, it will have its fulfillment in a covenant—in an alliance in which mankind is to give a perfect response of love to the love of the creator. God, the virginal being par excellence, is nonetheless to appear as a bridegroom. And the creature, although fallen and impure, is to be made finally the pure and exalted bride destined for a divine espousal.

Conversely, as we see it in the Song of Solomon, in the great epithalamion, Psalm 44: Human love, human marriage, including inseparably its bodily and spiritual aspects, is to be refined and elevated into a splendid image of the divine encounter and exchange of love between God and his own creature. And it will not be just an image, but clearly a mysterious participation of this most fundamental relationship between one creature and another in the most gratuitous, generous relationship that God intended to achieve between himself and his creatures in creating them.

There is a reason why God, becoming incarnate in his Son made man to make of us children of God, will be made male and not female. He will designate himself as a bridegroom coming to call and prepare the bride for that marriage of the lamb which therefore appears as the eschatological goal of the whole of human history. But that implies that the Church, the redeemed humanity, the perfected creation, will appear on its own side as supremely feminine, fully expressing and achieving what we can call the mystery of womanhood as a reflection upon the creature of the very divine mystery of that love of its creator manifested to us in Christ. Therefore, the eschatological Church—the Church of the last times, the perfected Church of whom Mary is a personal anticipation in the midst of history—is to become both virgin and spouse as Mary was to be virgin and mother at the source of all salvation, Virgin, to become the very spouse of the very son of God. This we can say is the ultimate mystery of which human sexuality was pre-ordained to be not only once again the image but the very channel of its realization in the history of man.

Henceforth there will be in the Church two inseparable images of its eschatological perfection which will be at the same time the complementary ways of its fulfillment. In consecrated virginity will be expressed and effectively anticipated the total dedication of the creature to her creator, which alone can achieve its perfect and definitive conjunction with him in love. In sacramental marriage will be expressed the inexhaustible fecundity of nature and of grace, of that conjunction, while the natural fecundity of created life will lend itself to be, as it were, the material of the spiritual and supernatural fecundity of uncreated life becoming our own life.

Far from what is so commonly said and repeated by people who know next to nothing of the history of Christian spirituality, that complementarity and inseparability of the two vocations of the sacramental marriage and the mystical virginity will make it characteristic of the greatest Christian ascetics that they will be, as the monk Paphnutius at the Council of Nicaea, the most convinced supporters of the sanctity of Christian sexuality. And the deepest theologians of monasticism, such as Gregory of Nyssa, will be also the most positive theologians of Christian marriage.

This is in such deep accordance with the nature of things that, in opposition to what we have heard said again and again in the last ten years, but in full agreement with what the reality of experience has told us afresh at the same time, it is when there is in the Church a proper understanding of virginity consecrated to Christ or more generally celibacy accepted freely for the coming of the kingdom of God, it is then that there is also a high and really positive view of Christian marriage. But when the first declines, immediately the second is threatened. The reverse is no less true. For a dedication to God in celibacy which would be connected with a fear of life, a lack of love, and not with the desire for life in its fullness and love in its divine integrity would have nothing to do with the Christian consecration of celibacy, either in the monastic life or in the apostolic ministry. And of that dignity and fecundity of love and of the capacity of the human being for becoming the bearer and partaker of the divine love itself, Christian marriage is more than the expression we need. It can be said to be the most convincing demonstration and anticipation in actual experience of what will be the ultimate fulfillment of faith passing into vision.

When all this has been said and seen, it should become clear that all the demands made by Christian ethics on the married couple are not the expression of I don't know what kind of crypto-Manicheeism, suspecting and trying to repress and as far as possible strangle the most basic human instinct and aspiration. Far from that, it may and should be seen that what Christian ethics excludes is only all that would impair and finally destroy the intrinsic beauty and fecundity of true human love between man and woman discovering all the significance of sexual love and above all its capacity, not only for expressing but for achieving participation in divine love itself incarnate in the whole of human nature. We have no difficulty any longer in seeing that whatever tends to deprive love of its generosity and fecundity is, in spite of appearances, not a liberation but a distortion and ultimately a corruption of that love.

This does not mean that preservation of its integrity and *a fortiori* its full growth will not imply many painful and costly sacrifices. But this is just the universal law of life in a fallen world, for a fallen nature called to a salvation which cannot be made its own without this cooperation, including what is the dispersion, the distortion of the authentically fruitful life, as the very condition of its growth and fecundity. But the most severe process of that kind will be acceptable in the very measure in which it is seen as just a prerequisite for the blossoming of that flower, for the maturing of those fruits which make up the very beauty of human love as it discovers in itself the emergence of divine love in the creature whom God has loved so much that he has given up his only Son so that it will not die but have life in abundance.

Such being the vision of faith which should spark the Christian couples in their common endeavor to fulfill and therefore, first of all, to keep undefiled their ideal of marriage, we have now to see the difficulties to overcome in order to keep the ideal in view and to actualize it within the concrete situation of today. At the same time, of course, we need to become fully aware also of what we can do practically, and especially what we clerics and religious should do to help them in their predicament.

On the first point, the difficulties: It is only too true that we have come back to a general state of society and public opinion which, far from buttressing the Christian ideal, much less contributing positively to its embodiment in daily existence, is at least as contrary to all that as were the pagan surroundings in which the first Christians found themselves in the beginning of Christian history. In our permissive society, in our civilization almost entirely channeled into a search for sensual enjoyment, it would seem at first sight that Christian married people have to run against the whole trend of the times, so that an ideal which is nonetheless in the right line of full human development will appear to call for no less than daily heroism not only to pursue it but even to keep it in mind.

Everything around us attempts to persuade us that the only natural way of life is to seek for nothing else but the maximum of sensual gratification with the minimum of moral privation. More precisely, the feminine body, not to say the whole of womanhood in spite of what we hear today of women's liberation, does not seem to appear to our contemporaries as anything more or anything other than an unlimited source of physical pleasure to be used as freely as possible without incurring any kind of moral obligation. That commonly is justified on the presupposition that the discoveries of Sigmund Freud make it incontrovertible that any other view of the matter implies an unhealthy repression which could not end except in neurosis.

Now it is very remarkable that Freud himself undoubtedly did not in the least interpret his work in that light. His correspondence with the Swiss reformed pastor Oscar Fister makes it especially conspicuous that he did not view his analysis of the human psyche as leading to a totally irresponsible exercise of sexuality, but to just the opposite —to a fully responsible and, for that, conscious mastery of it. The truth is that what is of the most lasting value in the work of Freud is precisely his view that sexual life, whether we want it or not, cannot be reduced to a mere search for pleasure. What he has put into full light is that sexuality is not just an enjoyable part of human life, easy to disassociate from the rest of it. On the contrary, wholeness of human life cannot be reached, according to him, as long as sex is not seen and exercised in its normal connection with all the aspects of human life and especially the deepest ones.

If this is so, the Freudian revolution should not end in sexual anarchy but in a renewed consciousness of the immense importance to us of not giving to sexuality any kind of biased or distorted development, but rather of assuming it in a most positive and constructive way, in such a way that its bearing on the whole of our integrated personalities is fully considered. Nothing could be, finally, a stronger confirmation to the Christian tradition properly understood.

However, we theologians and Christian moralists have much to do before we can re-express and, for that, rethink our teaching on sex in a way which will draw the full consequences of what I have just said. In order to come to that we cannot, of course, stop at the journalistic view of modern sexology, but must come to a fuller and more informed reflection upon what is, not without meaning, called depth psychology. But we have also and above all to draw from the Bible and the full Christian tradition much more than we are usually contented to do. Let us say frankly: Our common modern teaching that marriage is just a contract, with the sacrament of marriage itself being reduced to a secularization of the said contract, is radically unsatisfactory from this point of view, and that at both ends. It takes practically no account of the greatest and richest parts of the liturgical, patristic and biblical traditions. And it proves totally unable to offer a sound basis for the human and Christian ideal of marriage we have tried to outline.

For it is in the nature of a contract to be rescissible at will if the contracting parties come to an agreement on that. And even without going so far it is susceptible to being modified or reinterpreted in any way so long as they agree on the said interpretation or modification. But it has been recently emphasized in a text written by the French theologian Father Martelet and approved by the International Commission of Theologians that the very matter of the contract here is determined by the sacrament and by all that the sacrament evokes of the divine alliance in love between God and man. And, it should be added, this is based upon the very nature of human sexuality, itself appearing in the creation of man as a fundamental stepping stone for his future vocation to the supernatural life in Christ in the Church.

However, it is not enough for us to come, on these points, to a teaching much fuller and more explicit than found in our common handbooks: a right insistence on the impossibility of aiming realistically towards the fulfillment of the Christian ideal without rejecting all that which is opposed to it. However costly that fidelity may seem, it is contradicted not only by what is said and done in the world at large. Let us dare to say it is much more directly made incredible now and therefore unacceptable by too much of our present behavior within the Church. I mean the way in which we who pretend to teach to the laity their ideal, daily, now more than ever in the past, find all kinds of evasions to dispense with the following of our own ideal of a priestly or religious life.

Once again, the sanctity of married life and the sanctity of a life of apostolate or of monastic contemplation are most strictly inter-connected. Even this is not saying enough. We priests first, because we have to teach the true good life and the necessity of accepting all kinds of renunciations and free sacrifices in order to attend to it, should certainly be ready to accept for ourselves a rule more and not less exacting than that which we have to maintain for the laity. *A fortiori*, the religious who have or are supposed to have freely vowed a life of perfection in the pursuit of the fullness of Christian love through a maximum of generosity and self-detachment are to be the leaders par excellence of the married people through that path of sacrifice and self-denial which must be that of every genuine Christian.

But what do we see in the Church today? First, we priests are teaching the married people that they are to be faithful to each other until death, and then that they are, together, to repress their unruly desires in order not to reduce their mutual love to two egotisms. However, how can we still dare to do that when we seem to agree that we ourselves may freely, without any serious trouble, get from the Church dispensation from that entire dedication in celibacy to the service of God and man which was attached to our priestly consecration.

I know only too well the ready-made clerical answer: The laws of marriage are divine laws which cannot be compared with the law of celibacy for priests which is only a law of the Church from which the same authority which has established it can, as well, dispense. Yes, it can certainly do that. But does that mean that it does well ever to do it? Does that mean that those who had apparently accepted the obligation without qualms need only be no longer satisfied with it in order to get and enjoy their dispensation with a fully good conscience?

Recently I was watching television when a newsman was asking people in the street what they thought of those priests who now, with the consent of authority, leave their priesthood in order to marry. A most ordinary girl, who said openly she was not much of a Christian, answered: "As to me, I would have nothing to do with such a fellow. If he has not been able to be faithful to his Christ, do you think he could be faithful to a poor woman like me?"

Of course all preachers are humbly to say: Do rather what I teach than what I do. But how can they remain convinced and convincing teachers of any true love if they themselves as a class make it manifest that it is not for their own account a matter of life or death to be or not to be faithful to their own first love?

If this is true of the priests and their present way of too often handling their own obligations so lightly, what are we to say of the religious? Never in the past, since the first times of Christianity, have we seen so many religious clamoring to be dispensed from their vows and getting so easily their dispensations.

Has it not always been the teaching of the best Catholic theologians—the teaching of St. Thomas Aquinas especially —that a solemn and public vow, if it has been taken validly, is something from which, because it is a total surrendering of oneself directly to God, even the Church in its highest authority has no power to dispense? We tell married people that if we do not allow them to divorce or to profane that married love either by artificial contraception or abortion, it is because we clerics, even of the highest rank, have no power to dispense from a divine law. But then, how can we seriously, honestly, hope to have this accepted by people who have been called only to the ordinary and common way of Christian life as long as we are so proud or so lenient as to ask for or to concede the same kind of supposedly impossible dispensation when it is a matter of people having, it seemed, freely accepted what we call "a way of perfection"?

Do we not realize that we shall never regain our credibility in maintaining God's demands for the ordinary Christian while we seem so lightly to dispense from them the so-called perfect? I am afraid we will then make of our own preaching a disgusting joke; and we ourselves, clerics and monks or nuns, as long as we do not change our ways, must accept therefore to pass for dishonest and impudent fellows.

Let us conclude: Beautiful when seen in its proper light, and susceptible of evoking the most enthusiastic generosities, is certainly the Christian ideal of marriage. Wonderful are the gifts of life offered by Scripture and tradition to lead the Christian people in that way. And even more wonderful the graces opened to them by the sacrament they have received once for all, but from which they are to draw inexhaustible treasures all through their lives. But neither these lives nor those graces will be actually available to them if we priests, and first of all official teachers of the Christian truth, do not take much more trouble than we have until now to make that ideal fully expressed and realistically described to them. But above all, once again, the realization in true fact of the ideal of Christian marriage is not something that only the married people have to work out. If those who are supposed to have followed an even higher path, in celibacy consecrated to the apostolic ministry of an ascetic renunciation, freely vowed, do not appear to be much more genuinely concerned with their own ideal than they usually do today, we cannot hope that the laymen and laywomen of today will take seriously their own way of life. And it is not only a matter of our obscuring or weakening a teaching by the contradiction of our own practice. It is a matter of the common life of the body of Christ in which the supposedly weaker members cannot be expected to do the whole of their duty while the supposedly stronger ones seem mainly intent on finding ways of escape.

HANS URS VON BALTHASAR

Ephesians 5:21–33 and
Humanae Vitae:
A Meditation

I should like to offer a short meditation on the famous passage in the Letter to the Ephesians where Paul speaks of husband and wife and compares their relationship with the great mystery in which it is set, the mystery of the relationship of Christ with his Church. The passage is cited in *Humanae Vitae*, but is not commented on there at any length. Naturally this passage, taken by itself, cannot substantiate every doctrine and every demand contained in that encyclical; and yet, if we meditate deeply on Paul's words, we may come to perceive some of the central truths of the encyclical in a fuller light. Of course this meditation makes no pretense at exact exegesis of the text; many points in it are still very much in debate. But first we should look at the text itself.

> Submit to one another in the fear of Christ. Wives should be submissive to their husbands as if to the Lord because the husband is head of his wife just as Christ is head of his body the Church, as well as its savior. As the Church submits to Christ, so wives should submit to their husbands in everything.

Husbands, love your wives, as Christ loved the Church. He gave himself up for her to make her holy, purifying her in the bath of water by the power of the word, to present to himself a glorious Church, holy and immaculate, without stain or wrinkle or anything of that sort.

Husbands should love their wives as they do their own bodies. He who loves his wife loves himself. Observe that no one ever hates his own flesh; no, he nourishes it and takes care of it as Christ cares for the Church—for we are members of his body.

"For this reason a man shall leave his father and mother, and shall cling to his wife, and the two shall be made into one flesh."

This is a great mystery; I mean with reference to Christ and the Church.

In any case, each one should love his wife as he loves himself, the wife for her part showing respect for her husband.

The basic meaning is perfectly clear. Paul, or whoever the author may be—certainly someone close to Paul—is speaking here of Christian marriage, and he demands that Christian marriage be an unconditional following of Christ. He does not mean here that the two partners, as individual Christians, must each follow Christ; he makes it very clear that their marriage itself is to be a reflection of the relationship between Christ and the Church. These two relationships, man with woman, Christ with the Church, are closely intertwined, although (as we shall see) the place of Christ remains altogether unique and supreme. In marriage, as in all other human situations, Christ is our model, but a model to be *imitated*, not a model which can ever be duplicated.

Think of the hymn in Philippians. We are all to have the mind of Christ, who, though he was in the form of God, emptied himself, taking the form of man, and humbled himself even to death on the Cross. And for this reason God has exalted him above all creation and made him Lord of all. Now we cannot imitate Christ in these things: we cannot empty ourselves of the form of God, nor die on the Cross, nor be exalted above all creation. But, Paul tells us, we must have the mind of Christ. And we can have a mind by which each of us "thinks of others, in humility, as superior to himself" and makes himself "concerned with others' interests, not with his own" (Phil 2:3).

So too Christian marriage can take its structure from the relationship between Christ and the Church, even though that relationship presents an archetype which marriage can never perfectly resemble. Yet marriage can be lived psychologically within the rhythm of Christ's relations with the Church, because in truth and reality, Christian marriage *exists* only within the sphere of influence of the archetypical marriage of Christ with his Church. At the end of our text Paul adds: "This is a great mystery; I mean with reference to Christ and the Church." What precisely does Paul have in mind when he uses the word *mystery*? Does he refer to the marriage relation between man and woman (here expressly taken as physical), or does he use the word to signify the relationship between Christ and the Church alone, or is he referring back to the legend of Paradise (to which he has alluded in the previous verse), that Eve was fashioned from Adam's rib as prototype and parable of the Church's formation from Christ? We can leave this question open, because whatever the precise reference of the word *mystery*, it is evident that the passage as a whole refers to the entire complex, namely: conjugal relationships— that is, sexual relationships ordered to a higher purpose—

cannot exist outside the encompassing radiance of Christ's relationship with his Church, for which relationship the origin of Eve from Adam is and will always remain an eloquent parable. It is the mystery of Christ, though, which bestows upon marriage, as on all lesser relationships, its character of mystery.

We ought not to forget here that for Paul marriage is by no means the only way of being a follower of the Christ-mystery. In the First Letter to the Corinthians he points to the way of virginity and gives it preference when it means "being concerned about the Lord's affairs and seeking to please the Lord" (7:32). It is the way of Paul himself, and "I should like all men to be as I am. . . . To the unmarried and to the widows I say that they do well if they remain as I am" (7:7–8). In saying this, Paul is only repeating what Christ himself had lived and praised as a special charism. When lived in the spirit of Christ, the way of virginity is clearly a more direct imitation of Christ's relationship to the Church, and of his perfect fruitfulness. And yet, the Redeemer of the world is also the one who brings the order of creation to perfection, and he opens up marriage, grounded as it is in the order of creation, so that it becomes a way to follow him in a very specific manner.

The first sentence of our text brings us to the core of the statement: "Submit to one another in the fear of Christ." This fear of Christ certainly has nothing to do with a sense of terror which would alienate us from Christ. The *fear* Paul has in mind is the Old Testament sense of awe before the divine majesty of our Creator, Redeemer and Judge. "The fear of God is the beginning of wisdom" (Wis 1:7). So also is the fear of Christ the beginning of all Christian married life, a life which cannot be regulated by norms and laws of one's own invention, but only by the norm which is Christ himself and his manner of life.

It is wholly impossible for the injunction "Submit to one another" to apply only to the wives and not also to their husbands, since the same admonition is addressed even more frequently to Christians in general. We have already quoted the passage from Philippians, and in Galatians Paul repeats Christ's commandment: "Out of [Christian] love, place yourselves at one anothers' service" (5:13). Here the word is *douleuein*, which actually means "to perform the offices of a slave". And the First Letter of Peter demands: "In your dealings with one another, all of you should clothe yourselves in humility"—and this was said just after the rule had been given that the younger should submit to the older (5:5). The elders—the leaders—are to be no less humble than the young men; otherwise, how could they represent the Lord of the Church who, though our "Lord and Master", lived among us "as a servant" (Jn 12:13 ff.)? Now we can go on with our text.

> Submit to one another in the fear of Christ. Wives should be submissive to their husbands as if to the Lord, because the husband is head of the wife just as Christ is head of his body the Church, as well as its savior. As the Church submits to Christ, so wives should submit to their husbands in everything (Eph 5:21–24).

For the time being let us leave aside the troublesome statement that the husband is the head of his wife. Later on we shall have to ask to what extent this statement is historically conditioned, to what extent not. What concerns us now is a statement which is certainly *not* historically conditioned, namely, that Christ is the Head of the Church,

and indeed her Head because he is her Redeemer—*soter*.
This means that all members of the Church, men and
women, have every reason to submit to Christ. The fact
that Christ is here described as *Redeemer of his Body*, and not
Redeemer of his Bride or of his Spouse, may cause surprise;
but the words we expect follow soon. The well-known
image of Christ as *Head and Body* is given first so that it will
be evident that the Church owes her entire being to Christ.
The Church has first been brought forth from his fullness,
and then, in a second movement, she turns to him, herself a
living vessel for his fruitfulness. With regard to this, her
ultimate meaning, the Church is feminine. She is receptive
and nurturing; she gives birth to what she, as Christ's fruitfulness, has received from him. Israel was often enough
described as *bride* and *spouse* of her God, and the Church
continues and intensifies Israel's relationship with Yahweh,
being always feminine in reference to her God. Christians
from the first centuries to the Middle Ages always thought
of the Church as a woman and so represented her: *Mater
Ecclesia, Sponsa Christi*—and this despite the fact of the
hierarchy being composed solely of men. These men are
the agents of Christ-the-Bridegroom within the Church's
all-embracing femininity. Her femininity was even more
strongly emphasized in the Church of the Fathers and of the
Middle Ages by the fact that the Church was seen as united
with the Virgin Mother Mary and indeed was often made
almost identical with her. This identity flows from two
sources: First Mary, the virginal Mother, was appointed by
Christ on the Cross to be the Mother of all Christians and in
this sense to be his Bride. Second, through the Sacraments,
particularly Baptism and the Eucharist, the Church herself
bears all Christians as Christ's members in her womb and

nurtures them, thus becoming the mystical Mother of Christ.

Let us take a step further now and focus on the statement which follows: that Christ gave himself up (on the Cross) for his Church in order to make her a "spotless, holy and immaculate" Bride and so to present her to himself (5:27). And if we search out where it is that the Church fully meets this description, we again encounter the Woman who is the Immaculate One par excellence. We will also realize that, even as Mother of the Lord, Mary acquired her quality as *immaculata* from her Son, and indeed, from his Cross. As Mother, Mary clearly possesses and exercises authority over her Child; in Luke we read explicitly that "he submitted to them" (*hypotassomenos autois*, 2:51). But it is only by virtue of the Cross of her Son that Mary, redeemed by the Cross before the event, possesses the right and the capacity to bring up and shelter the Son of God.

Once we have truly seen and understood the role of Mary, we may turn to the problem presented to us by Paul's words: "Wives should be submissive to their husbands . . . because the husband is the head of his wife" (5:22–23). One might begin by objecting that this statement is obviously historically conditioned as Paul appears to demand submission only from those members of society who are, in fact, in an inferior position: women must submit to men, children to their fathers, slaves to their masters (Eph 6:1–5; Col 3:18, 20, 22). In so doing, he simply accepts the ancient social order as given; even, for example, when it assigns to fathers (and not to mothers) the responsibility of rearing their children. Then too, the ancient view of procreation may form a considerable part of the background of Paul's thought: the view, that is, that in procreation only the man plays an active, effective role, while the woman is merely passive and receptive; and that the nature of woman may be defined by a deficiency which makes her a *mas occasionatum*, a male *manqué*. (This view persisted even into High and Late Scholasticism.)

Now this idea of the inferiority of women in the social order was demolished and left behind long ago, precisely as a result of Christianity, which stresses the equal dignity of women. And the ancient theory of procreation has been thoroughly refuted by the insights of modern biology, which has realized that in the conception of a child, the woman's organism is just as active as the man's. Indeed, by reason of the long pregnancy, birth, the stages of feeding, and subsequent child care on the mother's part, we could say that the woman exhibits an activity which is significantly superior to the man's.

And there is more. I can only speak here as one interested in science, but with no special authority, but what I speak of is a pivotal finding of modern genetic research. Competent biologists have expressed the view that the basic embryonic structure of all living beings, including man, is primarily feminine, and the subsequent differentiation of the male arises from a tendency towards extreme formations, while the development of the female shows a persistence in the original balance.[1] If this is correct—and it certainly corresponds to an instinctive feeling that the womb of the *Natura naturans* is feminine—then we would have to reverse the scholastic definition of woman as a *mas occasionatum* and define the male, rather, as a *femina occasionata*, a woman

---

[1] Cf. Adolf Portmann, "Die biologischen Grundfragen der Typenlehre", in *Eranos*, 1974 (Leiden: Brill, 1977), 449–73.

manquée. However it may be, it is certain that the active power of the female organism as it forms the child in the womb, gives it birth and nourishes it, will (precisely if we contemplate it in the light of contemporary biology) make us see all created Being as essentially feminine when compared to the Creator God. From the beginning, matter requires the action of God: it is he who must bestow upon it the power to produce out of itself all the increasingly complex forms of life. And from this perspective we could say that the Church's relationship to Christ is the ultimate realization of the creature's relationship to God, since God has placed the creature in existence outside himself, and endowed it with the inner ability to nurture the seed it has received and, in turn, to send the seed out into its own life.

From all this we can now draw two conclusions which may answer the question whether the concept of man and woman displayed in our text is not perhaps historically conditioned and therefore dispensable.

The first thing that is said in our text is that the relationship between man and woman in marriage is an image of the relationship between Christ and the Church, and must pattern itself after the norm of that relationship. The decisive norm for the man-woman relationship is thus a *theological norm*, not a norm patterned on the social customs of a particular time. This point is very clearly impressed on us by the verse that follows: "Husbands, love your wives, as Christ loved the Church. He gave himself up for her" (5:25). And again we read: "In any case, each one should love his wife as he loves himself" (5:33, cf. 28), that is, as his own body, in the manner therefore in which Christ has loved his own body, the Church. This theological norm for the relationship between the sexes provides us with a sound guiding principle in applying the message of Paul to the problems of *Humanae Vitae*.

But before going on, we must make a second point that emerges from a comparison of the relationship between the sexes with the far superior archetype of the Christ-Church relationship. Christ does something that a husband can in no way do: Christ brings forth the Church from himself as his own fullness, as his Body, and, finally, as his Bride. By his self-surrender, he confers upon the Church the form and structure he desires, the life of the Holy Spirit that is a counterpart to his own life. The husband, on the other hand, encounters his wife as a separate person, with her own freedom and her own act of surrender to him—a freedom and a surrender which he does not create. The husband also realizes that, as we have seen, his wife posses-ses a feminine fruitfulness which is her own and stems even less from him.

Nevertheless, it does not seem to me that this simply invalidates the statement about the husband being the head of his wife. Prescinding from any and every social system (patriarchal or matriarchal) and from all theories of procrea-tion (ancient, scholastic or modern), it always remains true that in sexual intercourse it is the man who is the initiator, the leader, the shaper, while the woman's love—even if it is not passive, but just as active in its own way—is still essen-tially receptive. We could almost say—very naively—that, through the man, the woman is somehow awakened to herself, to the fullness of her feminine self-awareness. This initiative on the man's part is something primary which sets in motion the whole process of feminine fruitfulness. Such an order of things holds true even if we may smile at the incidental, marginal and transitory character of the male's function in procreation, a function which can certainly not be compared with Christ's extraordinary act of self-surrender.

But it still remains true that the absolute beginning lies in the progenitor—in the father—while the feminine principle, even as *Magna Mater* or as *Mother Nature*, can never be simply conceived as the beginning. In the Christian view of God, the begetting Father stands at the very source and origin of all things. This Father, to be sure, is incomparably superior to all earthly fatherhood. As a divine person, God the Father is eternally identical with his act of procreation, and of all creation only One is able to present to us a valid image of the Father: Jesus Christ, who creates the Church from the totality of his divine and human substance, which he surrenders on the Cross. The begetting power of Jesus Christ, which is what creates the Church, is his Eucharist, and over and beyond all times and places it is this Eucharist which makes the Church forever present. This power of Christ is the perfect image of the eternal Father precisely because neither Christ nor the Father holds anything back for himself or places any reservations on his own self-surrender; they have no fear of losing themselves through this perfect outpouring and lavishing of themselves. Unlike the man in the act of intercourse, Christ does not give away just a little of his substance. No, Christ gives away his entire substance, just as the eternal Father, in begetting the Son, makes over to the Son his entire divine substance, and then again both of them give this substance over to the Holy Spirit, without division, in an act of communal love.

In the act of procreation, the man represents but a distant analogy to this trinitarian and christological event. But it is an analogy nonetheless; and this analogy allows us to acknowledge, even today, the truth contained in the statement that the husband is the head of his wife. The husband, however, must be aware that his action stands under a norm, under a Head, just as Christ, in his self-surrender to the Church, is ever mindful that in his action in the world he is carrying out his mission: to represent the goodness of the Father who gives of himself eternally. So Paul says in the First Letter to the Corinthians: "You should know that Christ is the Head of every man, and the man is the head of the woman, and God the Head of Christ" (11:3). And if the word *head* appears awkward here, we could instead say: that superior reality which at the same time bestows and releases power, but always along with it a norm according to which that power is to be exercised.

From all this we have gained one general insight: For the Christian husband and for the Christian wife, the norm of their sexual relationship is a *theological* one, namely, the relationship between Christ and the Church. We could say that this holds true for all *non*-Christians as well, only they know nothing of this norm and cannot therefore consciously pattern themselves after it. It must suffice here to speak of this norm in so far as it concerns Christians. We cannot examine here the ways in which conscious conformity to this norm, conscious participation in Christ's activity, makes Christian marriage a sacrament. And our text from Paul does not deal with this question, although it does speak of the great mystery (*sacramentum*). But the word *sacramentum* here refers to the whole structure; it refers to the relationship between Christ and the Church and to this relationship as the all-embracing sphere within which the marriage relationship between husband and wife has its existence.

Before we conclude by reflecting explicitly on *Humanae Vitae*, we must insert an additional observation that seems important to our text. We have previously spoken of the ephemeral nature of the man's contribution in setting in motion the great process of feminine fruitfulness. And yet, in the sexual act, the man does give from what is his and, if he is to stand under the norm of Christ, he *ought* not only give *something* of what is his, but must rather surrender *his very self*, just as the eternal Father surrenders his very self and everything which is his in order to beget the Son. If the husband does this, he will come all the closer to Christ, who by his self-surrender fashions his Mystical Body for himself.

This is why our text also says: "Husbands should love their wives as they do their own bodies", for no one hates his own body, but rather "nourishes it and takes care of it as Christ cares for the Church." And then we are referred to the great passage in Genesis where we read that: "For this reason a man shall leave his father and mother, and shall cling to his wife, and the two shall be made into one" (Eph 5:28b–31). For Christ this means that on the Cross and in the Eucharist he gives of his Flesh and his Blood so unreservedly that in what results from this self-surrender—that is, in the Church as a separate being outside himself—Christ finds himself again. This rediscovery of himself in the Church would not be possible if Christ had only half-given himself and half-kept himself back. If we reflect from this perspective on the husband's part in the sexual act, we will see that he can do justice to the commandment to love his wife as his own body *only* if he hands himself over to her unconditionally, so that from now on he can recognize in her all that he has surrendered; that is, his entire self.

We can now sense the magnitude of what is demanded. What man can do justice to it? Truly, a supernatural measure of selflessness is required in order to bring a man to such love as this, possessive as he is by nature and rendered selfish in his sexuality by sin. Man *needs* woman in order to release and satisfy himself, even though he may also feel the impulse of love, strong or weak, genuine or imaginary. And very often he loves the woman as his own body, which he nourishes and looks after, in an egotistical sense, a sense which is the exact opposite of what our text means. The Middle Ages, with its realistic bent of mind, spoke of the *remedium concupiscentiae* ("a remedy for lust"), in stern contrast to our modern sexual theories, which are mostly unrealistic and idyllic, and trivialize sexuality. Paul is himself a realist when in the First Letter to the Corinthians he recommends: "Those who do not have the strength to abstain ought to marry, for it is better to marry than to burn [with desire]" (7:9).

In love, as in fidelity, the woman has an easier time of it. As we have said, she is creatureliness itself with regard to God, and with regard to Christ she is the very image of the Church. The woman is not called upon to represent anything which she herself is not, while the man has to represent the very source of life, which he can never *be*.

We now take up the question of *Humanae Vitae* by affirming that the highest of all relationships, that between Christ and the Church, is by its nature a fruitful one. The notion of fruitfulness is basic in the New Testament: just think of the parables of growth, the parable of the barren tree which must be cut down, and particularly the parable of the vine and the branches. The Church herself embodies the fruitfulness of Christ, and together with him she is again to bear fruit—"fruits of the Spirit" (Gal 5:22), "fruits of the light" (Eph 5:9), "fruits of justice" (Phil 1:11, James 3:18). It goes without saying that the concept of fruitfulness brings us into a sphere that affects every Christian, without distinction between the married and those who have consecrated their virginity to God. We have only to think of Mary, whose physical fruitfulness is itself the fruit of her faith and her virginity. And yet it is from the fruitfulness of Christ and the Church that the model for the married state may be drawn. For the source of this fruitfulness lies in the fact that no limits whatsoever are imposed on self-surrender either on Christ's part or on that of the Church. Christ's eucharistic self-surrender on the Cross is absolutely unreserved: reckless, we might say. He abandons himself to the abyss of sin; he gives himself to those who are unworthy of him, a gift symbolized by the morsel he hands to Judas. And in Mary, at least, there is a loving readiness to receive, equally unreserved. Her assent means that she can be led in any direction, even into places and situations which she neither knows nor suspects. It is precisely this attitude which is the source of all Christian fruitfulness, not the performance of any calculated and well-planned "good works" whatever.

We find a striking comparison of these two attitudes in the narrative of the supper at Bethany. On one hand we have Mary's anointing of Jesus, an expression of her boundless surrender to him. And Jesus takes up her surrender and makes it part of the divine plan of salvation, an anointing for his Passion. Mary takes on the role of the loving Church, ministering to Jesus in acceptance of his eucharistic self-surrender—*personam Ecclesia gerens*, as the Fathers say. On the other hand, we have Judas: "What is the good of this waste? Why wasn't the oil sold, and the money given to the poor? It was worth more than three hundred denarii." Sound thinking, one might say, but the Gospel-writer unmasks its secret egotism.

Let us turn back now to human marriage. The union of husband and wife means more than merely physical fruit-fulness, the begetting of children; it means spiritual fruitful-ness as well, total surrender to each other. Now the con-junction in man of the physical and the spiritual involves an inherent ambiguity, for these two aspects of his life are altogether inseparable. Man is at once body and spirit. He is a member of an animal species in which procreation, birth and death are interdependent; and at the same time he is person and spirit, superior to all other species. Because of this conjunction of animal and spiritual he cannot remain a person without remaining a member of his species. There-fore, he cannot divert a species-oriented function from its inherent purpose solely in order to satisfy his own personal desires. Or rather, he *can* do so, but not without schizo-phrenically splitting his own inner organic unity. For when he acts in this way, he sets his own personal limits on a function of the human species, a function with its own inner finality. Ostensibly, he limits his fertility in this manner so that he can give fuller emphasis to the limitless, personal side of his being. But in so doing he obviously introduces an element of calculation and limitation into an act which is meant to be the symbolic expression of an unconditional love between man and woman.

All of us are aware of the social problems to which the indissoluble duality of man's sexual nature can lead, both at the family level and at the wider level of state and society as a whole. It should not surprise us then that as their problems grow more severe, men are easily persuaded to adopt the lesser of two evils: that is, to introduce calculation into an act which in its perfection is beyond all calculation. As the encyclical states, one can find all sorts of excuses for such behavior. People take as their ultimate argument the fact that the distinctive part of man's nature is his ability to master the physical and biological world, and shape it to his own needs and purposes.

When men no longer see themselves bound by the norm of that love which exists between Christ and the Church, one can hardly convince them that their arrogation of full power to regulate the procreative function puts all truly personal love between man and woman in serious jeopardy. And the task is all the more difficult because in the present post-Christian era most men have already lost all vision of the unique and eternal dignity of the person. This loss of vision is equally evident in both halves of the world—in that half where the individual is seen as a mere function of economic laws, and in the other half, too, where the word *freedom* is still written large, but where the fundamental sciences of life are psychology and sociology.

The Christian couple today lives in a society beset with dangers and uncertainties unprecedented in human history, and they will have no easy life if they desire to make the absolute love of Christ and his Church the rule of their lives. But this love itself will guide the couple along a path they can follow.

The wellspring of the whole Christian life is certainly the spirit of faith, hope and love, a will to engage in a total, not a partial, imitation of Christ, an enduring endeavor to remove the barriers against Christ which we are always putting up, sinners and self-worshippers that we are. And when a man and a woman live this sort of life, keeping

before their eyes Christ's eucharistic love and Mary's assent, they will inevitably find themselves restrained from
debasing their acts of married love; acts which are intended
by their very nature to express an unlimited and self-giving
love.

But does not society itself impose such limitations on
married love with irresistible force? Does society not exert
such moral pressure on married people that they cannot
follow the norms of Christ unreservedly? The encyclical
answers these questions by saying that before society began
to make such demands, nature itself had come to man's aid
by establishing a periodic rhythm in the days of a woman's
physical fertility. (I emphasize the word *physical*, for her
spiritual fertility, which is supernatural and flows out from
grace, has no periods.) And there is all the difference in the
world between utilizing one's awareness of the periods of
infertility, and arrogating to oneself the right to impose
radical restrictions on fertility by the use of artificial contraception.

Many see little difference here. And perhaps there is little
difference, so long as man views himself as an entity which
invents itself and regulates itself: *homo technicus*. Were this
view of man the truth, no limits at all could be set on his
manipulation of his own nature.

But the difference is great to the eyes of any man or
woman who thinks as a Christian. For in using the infertile
days they are not setting bounds to their love. Otherwise,
one would have to say that intercourse in the full Christian
sense is impossible after a woman's change of life. Married
persons who think as Christians set no barriers between the
two objects of marriage: procreation and the expression of
mutual love. They let the two stand together, the physical

side with its own proper laws, and the personal side. One's awareness of the opportunities provided by nature does not mean that one is imposing calculation on the inner spirit of love.

Let us end with this observation. For sexuality as Christians understand it—sexuality that takes as its norm the relationship between Christ and his Church—Christ's words hold true: "Let him grasp it who can." But Christ is saying something more here than that very few men and women will actually grasp his doctrine. He is issuing us a challenge to serious endeavor, the same challenge, essentially, that rings through the whole of the Gospel: Take up your cross every day, sell all you possess, and do not cheat as did Ananias and Sapphira. Why should the sexual area alone offer no challenge to the Christian? Sexuality, even as *Eros*, is to be an expression of *Agape*, and *Agape* always involves an element of renunciation. And only by renunciation can the limits that we set on our own self-surrender be transcended.

I think that Christians alone can understand the challenge posed by *Humanae Vitae*, and even Christians only to the degree that they strive to follow Christ as married persons, and keep his example before their eyes with ever-increasing devotion. For all of them—men and women—are, after all, sons and daughters of the Church, who owes her existence to Christ, and who raises her eyes to him with reverence and awe, his loving Bride (Eph 5:33).

JEAN GUITTON
Eros and Agape

During the five years I spent in captivity during World War II, I prepared a book that I published in 1946, *L'Amour Humaine* (*Human Love*). Although I was, of course, deprived at that time of all feminine contact, I still had the opportunity of talking with some six thousand comrades, most of whom were married. In rereading it, almost fifteen years later, I noticed imperfections and decided that I should add an appendix on *divine love* in its relation to *human love*.

This question is difficult and profound. In 1940, as a prisoner, I had searched for a book that would explain love to me from a synthetic, integral, all-embracing point of view. As I did not find such a book (at least not in the camp library), I decided to try writing it myself. I soon realized that it was impossible to find a *perfect* book on love because whenever a subject is studied (in this instance, human sexuality), it is studied from a particular point of view, by a particular method and in a particular language. This point of view, this method, this language have the effect of both illuminating and obscuring the subject *at the same time*.

One of the problems of modern physics results from the instruments used to study a particle of matter. They make the particle visible yet alter it *in the process*. It is quite the same with thought processes. It seemed to me that there are three languages for speaking about love—three languages that are at once illuminating and obscuring. The first of these languages is the *lyrical*, romantic language found in novels and poems. Love is represented as an ecstasy. This language is beautiful (as we shall see presently), but it is imperfect when applied to conjugal love, which is not an endlessly renewed passion but an evolution that endures through time.

The second point of view on love is the *juridical* one, which attempts to preserve the purity of love by condemning its aberrations and by considering it primarily from a negative standpoint, as offense, fault and sin. How many books, how many instructions, how much advice have we all received that accustomed us from childhood to regard the things of love as forbidden. Clearly this point of view, although fundamentally just, does not go to the heart of the problem.

A third point of view is the *scientific*, empirical, medical one that sees love as a biological activity, a natural function to be regulated by hygiene. This is also the perspective of psychoanalysts who disclose the underlying determinants of sexuality. The scientists and technicians overlook the fact that love poses all the problems of ethics because the biological act is permeated by the spirit. I sought a higher point of view that would allow me to make use of all these studies and languages in order to come to grips with human love intellectually.

One of the difficulties in discussing the subject of love is that the same word is used to designate very different things. In common usage the word "love" denotes the lowest activity (to *make love*). Yet if you read St. Francis de

Sales, you realize that love also denotes the highest, most mystical and most divine of all activities since love is the action that places us in immediate relation to God. There is good reason for this ambiguity. An obscure truth is actually hidden in this ambiguity of the word love. It is this truth that I would like to set in relief by showing you, in a way both old and new, the relationship between sexual love and divine love.

ANIMAL SEXUALITY AND HUMAN SEXUALITY

The first question I addressed in studying human love was a simple question that occurs to all men—one that has been raised before, continues to be raised and will again be raised in the future. I sought to understand the curious difference that exists between animal sexuality and human sexuality. (The technical works on the sexuality of monkeys, for instance, are very interesting.)

This relationship is interesting to study for all who wish to consider man—because the mystery of man is that he is a *loving animal*. Man has the same biological functions as the animal. And yet veterinarians are not physicians. Because it is assumed, refined and integrated into a higher order (called "reason and love", the "attribute of man", the "resemblance to God"), the biological function common to both the animal and man (such as digestion or reproduction) no longer has the same form or the same purpose. And when reason is added to animality, when the *logos* of man is added to the *bios* of the animal, we get a being at once sublime and mad. We see it in our own time with the progress in science: reason makes man the master of nature. But at the same time, science is capable of destroying humanity by pollution or by an atomic accident.

What is true of reason is even more true of love. When the sexual being called "animal" is assumed by this fire, this form, this higher finality called love, then he is capable at the same time of elevating or degrading himself. And in a general way, it could be said of the "loving animal" that is man what Baudelaire said of the albatross: "his giant wings prevent him from walking."

What are the fundamental differences between man and animal? The first difference is that for the animal, the two biological functions necessary for the survival of the species, preservation and reproduction, are automatic, compulsive, obligatory. The animal cannot prevent itself from eating. The animal does not *fast*. Nor can it keep from breeding (at much more regular periods than man). Now, curiously enough, when these two functions are assumed into the reason/love context—when the animal becomes man—the digestion, a function affecting the individual's survival, is nearly as compulsive as the animal's. But strangely enough, when reproduction is assumed by reason/love, it becomes a free function. Man can choose not to exercise his reproductive function and still live, live well, and often, in truth, enjoy an even higher freedom.

Here we have something striking which shows how the assumption of a biological function by reason/love transforms this function. We who talk so much about "freedom"—we can say that it is really through the reproductive function, and by the power man has over this function (in not exercising it or in exercising it in a reasonable way), that his free will manifests itself.

This is, moreover, why what all the libertines of the world repeatedly tell us—that man is as constrained by his reproductive function as by his digestive function—is patently false, since we see ascetics and the chaste live and live well!

The second observation is that the animal only has *needs*, while with us, need is transformed into desire. And when need (which is delimited, finite) is transformed into desire, infinity is added to it. To put it another way, sexual need almost changes its nature when it becomes human desire, passionate desire. With passionate lovers, desire can become all consuming up to the point of delirium and sometimes to the point of death. You have only to read Tristan and Isolde. But all those among us who have loved know that the need is minute in proportion to those overtones in the imagination that color the glandular phenomenon in order to give it the infinite resonances that constitute both the misery and the grandeur of love.

Another observation is that the sexual need of the animal is an abstract, general need. The dog does not love *a* dog, it loves *some* dog (and when man debases himself to the point of animality, it is not Simone, but *some woman*, any woman). Such is the metaphysical status of prostitution. The wolf loves some wolf; the bull loves some cow and not a particular cow. Such is the greatness and the cross of human love, its passion, in the marvelous ambivalence of this word. And the mystery of sexuality (what Pascal observed in his discourse on the "passions and love") is that sexual desire, which already contains the infinite since it adds human infinity to the biological finitude, this sexual desire, instead of addressing itself to any partner whatever, limits itself to a particular being. Pierre loves Françoise and only Françoise! All other women who could be introduced to him no longer interest him. It is only Françoise whom he loves. That reminds me of a friend of mine, now dead, who had loved a girl about whom I had made some inquiries. I told him that the information was not good. Let's say that the young girl was named Hélène. My friend replied to me: "I would rather be unhappy all my life with Hélène than happy with another." This was, in humorous (and tragic) terms, the characteristic of human love—this absolute fixation of one being upon another—that introduces us to the mystical.

EROS AND AGAPE

I characterize the reflections I have just made by a single word—this word is EROS. There is in man a vital instinct which is humanized by the presence of infinity, by its concentration on one personality, its restriction to one being—this instinct I call EROS.

I do not give the word *Eros* the same meaning conferred on it in speech by the words "eroticism" and "erotic". I define *Eros* very precisely as the sexual instinct (the "libido", if you wish) *in so far as it is assumed by love in this composite being called man*. In opposition to this instinct that I call *Eros*, each of us has another feeling: that of closeness, a protective sense, a friendly and benevolent feeling that unites us with others, that creates a reciprocal exchange between others and ourselves, that allows us to build families, to taste the joys of friendship, that is the cement par excellence of society and of all *politics* in the noblest sense. The Greeks had two words for this latter feeling: PHILIA, which means "love", or else the word AGAPE, which means tender, reverent love and which we would have to translate as DILECTION if this word were not a little outdated.

Consequently, two forces oppose each other in human nature: on the one hand, *Eros*, which is an ardent and exclusive feeling (that the Hebrews actually called "jealousy") and which is expressed by the metaphor of flame; and on the other, a feeling that might be called *Friendship* (usually translated as *Agape*), which is a feeling that is not ardent like flame but sweet like light, not exclusive like jealous passion, but, on the contrary, a far-reaching, universal feeling. It is the sentiment with which a man loves another man, the sentiment with which friends are made. It is with this feeling of *Agape* that a person loves his father and mother, his students, his fellow citizens and other men.

Obviously, then, the philosopher is faced with the problem of how to distinguish between *Eros* and *Agape*.

It could be said that *Eros* designates love in so far as love finds its nourishment in transformed, transfigured, purified sexuality and that friendship, on the contrary, is a sentiment that has nothing to do with sexuality, that is built outside of all sexuality.

When it was necessary to give a name to the Eucharist, it was first called *Agape*. When St. John wanted to define God (*Theos*), he could have said *Theos Eros esti*, or, *God is ardent Love*; he could have said *Theos Philia esti*, or, *God is Friendship*. But he preferred to say (and we are about to understand why): *Theos Agape esti. Deus Caritas est*. It could have been said *Deus Amor est! God is Love!* But no, it was said *Deus Caritas est*—God is tender love, pure love, concerned love, universal love; God is charity; *God is Agape*.

Having said that, I am faced with a great problem—that of determining which feelings, which energizing and spiritual forces are the ones capable of leading me to God.

To strengthen my bond with God, am I going to use *Eros* or *Agape*? Let's open the Bible and listen to the supreme commandment. "You shall love your God with all your spirit." You shall love! It is not a question of loving God with *Eros*, it is a question of loving God with *Agape*. And yet we are told that it is necessary to love God with all our heart, with all our spirit, with all our strength.

In order to reach God, is it necessary to condemn *Eros*? Or, on the contrary, is it necessary to use *Eros* in order to love God? And then, how?

To reach God, would it not be necessary to find a method that would consist of collecting the latent energy in *Eros* in order to transform *Eros* into *Agape* and to charge *Agape* with that exclusivity contained within the precept: "You shall love your God with all your heart, with all your soul; you shall love your God jealously because God loves you jealously!"

In the Bible, in reading Hosea and the prophets, it can be seen that God loves Israel as a lover loves his beloved, not as a master loves his slave. God is a jealous God. God wants the people of Israel to love him as a woman loves her husband. This leads us to think that it is necessary to transmute or raise *Eros* into *Agape* in a certain way that I am going to suggest. It implies that in sexuality itself there is something capable of sublimation. It also leads to a very high opinion of marriage as a means of loving God.

This sublimation of *Eros* in *Agape* under the influence of grace particularly characterized the great mystics. They loved God in an impassioned, total, exclusive, ardent, reciprocal, inflamed, nuptial, ravishing, transverberating and sometimes even deadly way.

If you study St. Catherine of Genoa, a very great mystic and the inspiration of one of my masters, the Baron von Hügel, an English Catholic; if you study St. Teresa of Avila, whom Pope Paul VI made a Doctor of the Church; if you study St. John of the Cross, you see that the mystics love God in a way that is not so much "agapic" as "erotic", taking this word in its noblest and purest sense. The language often used by the mystic to express his feelings in his encounter with God is the language of passionate love. I remember that my parents, with good reason, kept the writings of the mystics in a locked cupboard because they thought they might disturb me. Finally, the mystics use nuptial language to speak of their union with God, describing it as a spiritual marriage. If you look at Bernini's statue representing St. Teresa's transverberation by the archangel, you will notice that it evokes a spasm of love and of suffering. The study of the mystics leads one to think that there is a profound and nearly inexpressible reality there; I am going to try to study it delicately. Let the Spirit propose angelic words and the seraphic spirit, for I wish to express something luminous, pure and burning.

When I was twenty-five years old, I translated the Song of Songs from Hebrew with the help of my professor, Mr. Pouget. How many hours I spent over the Song of Songs!

After finishing my translation, I took it to Jerusalem, to Fr.
Lagrange, who was kind enough to accept it. It appeared in
the collection of *Biblical Studies* in 1934. I had been struck by
the (let's say the word) "erotic" character of the Song of
Songs, and it still surprises me. There is no nuptial song
more ardent nor (in a certain sense) less inclined toward
procreation. Mr. Pouget told me, however, that the young
woman's desire to taste "mandrakes" did in fact signify her
desire for a child since the mandrake was considered an
aphrodisiac by the Jews—a "pro-conceptive", not a contraceptive. But apart from this single verse, there is no
reference at all to progeny in the Song. It is the song of the
betrothed, or rather the song of the first months of married
life, it is the song wherein love is all—and a reciprocal love
that will be fruitful as well, if Yahweh wishes. The difference between the Song of Songs and the nuptial songs (of
Mesopotamia, Assyria or Egypt) that might have inspired
the Song's author is that in the nuptial songs, the bridegroom is master and the bride is only a privileged slave,
while in the Song of Songs, the love of the bridegroom for
the bride equals that of the bride for the bridegroom. The
woman loves as much as the man and the man as much as
the woman. One truly senses them to be equal in admiration, in joy, in pain when separated.

Mystics—probably the Jewish mystics at the time the
Song was written, around three hundred years before Jesus
Christ, and the Christian mystics since then (particularly
St. John of the Cross)—say that the Song of Songs cele-
brates the love of the soul for God, the love of the virgin
for Christ, the love of consecrated souls for God.

We have not previously paid enough attention to the fact
that the Song of Songs, in its original meaning, celebrated

nuptial love, that it is even the most beautiful song that could exist for exalting what this love contains in its fullness. In what I wrote on the Song of Songs, I supported the thesis (which I still firmly believe) that in the Song there are three characters: a young peasant woman who is loved by King Solomon, who offers her all his wealth and also power and even the opportunity of being his beloved wife and, on the other hand, a young shepherd, a poor peasant like herself. And the sense of the Song is that the young woman prefers the love of her husband or fiancé, who is the young shepherd, to the love of the king (whom she could have married without sin according to Jewish law): "If the king had given me the great city of Paris and had made it necessary for me to leave the love of my life, I would say to King Henry, take back your Paris, I prefer my heart's love."

Such is the original and primary meaning of this theme always and everywhere popular.

The Canticle ends with a marvelous phrase on the subject of love: "The flames of love (it speaks here of conjugal love) are the burning heat of fire; they are the flames of Yahweh!" The flames of love are the flames of God; in Greek, the word is not *Eros* but *Agape*. This idea, which is expressed in the Song of Songs, has still not been fully developed two thousand years later.

I would like to insert here a consideration of the role of mystics in the Church, remembering Joubert's thought on piety, which, he said, is necessary to compensate for what is too intellectual in our relationship with God. When religion makes the fatal mistake of becoming too juridical, too logical, too sociological, too cerebral, God raises up mystics, the new prophets. When the medieval world was in danger of growing cold—St. Francis and St. Dominic. Or again, to compensate for Jansenism—Margaret Mary, Grignion de Montfort, the Sacred Heart, Marian devotion. If the cerebral dominates the Church too much after Vatican II, I believe mystics will again appear.

Now mysticism, from the point of view I have adopted in this essay, is an infusion of divine *Eros* into *Agape*. Read chapter 5 of the third book of the *Imitation* and you will understand what I mean.

SEXUALITY—A SOURCE OF SPIRITUAL ENERGY?

In pursuing this traditional view, I am sometimes led to wonder if sexuality might not be a source of spirtiual energy, and if one of the aspects of *Casti Connubii*—that is to say, of reasonable, loving, Christian marriage—is not found there.

This touches on the theme that Father de Lubac has treated in commenting upon Father Teilhard de Chardin— the "Eternal Feminine". Here, those two geniuses, Dante and Goethe, meet. This is the idea that inspired the *Divine Comedy*. All of Dante's philosophy, his theology, even his politics, result from a love he conceived for a person who had only begun to mature (she was scarcely a young girl) whom he had seen only twice up to the time that Beatrice faded before the Virgin and Dante revealed the secret of the cosmic system: the energy that sets the spheres in motion is love. At the end of the second *Faust*, Goethe says that "Eternal Womanhood draws us toward the heavens."

In our own times, Father Teilhard, as Father de Lubac has shown, revives these views. Teilhard thought that sexual energy, cleansed of its sin, was a unifying force of profound purity, a perceptible method of synthesis. He said one day that "Purity is the manner in which the ultimate center of their coincidence appears above two individuals who love each other."

In our culture, which is so often aphrodisiac because we have allowed concupiscent *Eros* to prevail over sublimated *Eros*, this narcissistic *Eros* has become a force for division, dissociation, false exaltation, and annihilation. It is a fire that devastates and devours like a nuclear holocaust.

Is it not possible to reverse this trend, as they are trying to do for the atom, to use this energy of purified *Eros* for higher purposes? This is a difficult task. First it is necessary to fight against evil and temptation. But at this point, let's be careful not to *repress Eros* when what would be necessary is to sacrifice it—by which I mean: to render it sacred, in carrying it higher (without annihilating it) to *sublimate* it. A purely negative fight against instinct not accompanied by the act of sublimation (which would be *ablation* without also being *oblation*) is a possible cause of anguish and neurosis. Psychoanalysis teaches us this.

EVOLUTION AS GOD SEES IT

Let's place ourselves higher still and consider the evolution of living beings from the viewpoint of God, who sees it reduced to an indivisible instant (a thousand years, O Eternal One, are as a day for you) and who thus beholds in a single glance both the beginning and the end of the species living on the planet.

There are two ways of judging an evolution. One is man's (that of the scholar or biologist), which follows a horizontal development. For example, one might consider the first cell from which we were produced, then the embryo, the newborn, the child, the adult, etc. Or perhaps first the invertebrates, then the vertebrates, the mammals, the primates, the great apes, man. . . . Clearly, the Absolute Being does not proceed like this. He does not proceed from the beginning but from the end, from the consummation. The evolutional order, that detaches, divides and succeeds itself in time, is for him just the reverse of the real order in the eternal creative thought. God first sets the goals, the sublime moments, the last judgments, the ultimate plenitudes.

He wants gods, saints, a holy city, a people of priests, the elect united by bonds of love. He wants *heaven*. And so that there might be the mystical heaven, he makes the physical heaven and the planets where life can appear. Let us begin, says God, with the galaxy. This regressive analysis, which goes from the end to the means, appears illusory and arbitrary to the modern intelligence that is losing the understanding of the essence and of the end. It is incontestable that what was fundamental was sexuality as it appeared in animal nature, that is to say, the momentary coming together of two individuals for the purpose of procreation, with all its retinue of instinctive impulses and sensible satisfactions. Love was grafted onto this sexuality as if by accident. In other words, a purely physical process was, little by little, refined, transformed and intellectualized by a series of accidents and by the gradual effect of society and civilization up to the moment when love, this product of sexuality, was able to free itself from its stem. Thus love, the last term of the series—animal sexuality, human sexuality, love—would be produced by a refinement of the preceding phases. When this line of reasoning is accepted, one is forced to admit that the superior term of the series is derived from the inferior by a set of favorable accidents. But is the perfection of fortunate variations for the benefit of our species not too much to ask of chance without assuming a guardian spirit of the species who directs the accidents? And in that case, would it not be better to say (however inadequate this phrase may be) that nature works to realize love? Now for that, it is necessary to have individuals capable of knowing and seeking one another, who are thus distinct even though similar, and who, while remaining separate and incommunicable in their essence, can nevertheless unite in a way that makes them one. If such is the case, then sexuality appears as a means of realizing love.

The change of perspective is radical. It is no longer love that is conceived as an artificial and accidental consequence of sexuality. It is, on the contrary, sexuality that appears to be a helpful tool for arousing and maintaining love in a society made up of distinct individuals bound up in matter and corporeality.

This difference in perspective shifts the areas of obscurity. In the doctrine of horizontal evolution, what is most difficult to justify is *human* sexuality, which seems an accidental by-product. From now on, it is *animal* sexuality that becomes the most inexplicable, for it seems a useless luxury. Since the animal lacks interiority, what can be the meaning of these bizarre copulations, from the toad to the ape, that do not ensure any symbiosis of individuals or any communion of consciousness? This is the impression we receive when we observe the coupling of beasts, which immediately seems strange, caricatured and obscene to us. This is also the feeling of a number of biologists who see animal sexuality as an onerous complication that is difficult to explain from the standpoint of an orthodox Darwinian because it is of no benefit in the fight for survival. But if we assume that the ultimate purpose of the vital impulse is to make man (as Elohim said on the sixth day), then the antecedent stages—which are only preparatory passages that do not contain their final goal within themselves—must necessarily present characteristics that could only seem absurd to the scientific intelligence that methodologically refuses to relate them to the definitive end that alone explains them fully. At least, this must be so if it is true that the animal stages of coupling prepare the substructures, the conditions for human love, for monogenetic and conjugal love.

SEXUALITY, THE WAY TOWARD THE LOVE OF GOD

To summarize, then, God wanted to create beings who would be eternally united with him in his love! He wanted to prepare biological and thinking beings for that sweet and burning, motionless and endlessly progressive state of life—my definition of heaven.

In order to obtain this ultimate end in a slow, sure, quiet way, in stages prepared temporally over the course of the ages, God created sexually differentiated beings, animals whom he divided in two—female and male—two individuals separate in body but drawn toward each other. He perfected this mechanism of attraction between two com-

plementary beings by giving the nervous system a faculty of
freedom and inhibition. He thus prepared humanity for the
purpose of promoting, by means of marriage, the growth
of love, which itself allows temporal beings to prepare
themselves for eternal union.

Parenthetically, I would like to relate a conversation I had
with Bergson around 1930. We were talking about the Song
of Songs. I had brought him a copy of my book. He took it
in his hands and said to me:

"Yes, the Song has made me reflect. I think that conjugal
union, for Jews as well as for Christians, cannot be ex-
plained in a purely biological or social way." He con-
tinued, "Look at the Greeks. They recognized two types of
women: the woman of the streets and the matron. Venus
Aphrodite and the mother of the citizens. But they did not
know the beloved woman, Uxor."

He said to me, "I was very struck to see that mystics very
naturally use the language of nuptial love to describe their
mystical states. I wonder if it would not be necessary to say
this: what has begun is mystical love! What has begun is the
ardent love of the soul for God. It is this mystical love that
has made conjugal love possible. So that when mystics use
the language of conjugal love, they are doing nothing but
recovering their own possession."

I had the impression that I was listening there to a voice
that was absolutely different if not diametrically opposed to
that of Freud. And I recognized the necessity of choosing
between Freud and Bergson.

A little later, opening Virgil to the ninth book of the
Aenead, I found again these verses that I had greatly liked in
my adolescence, devoted as it was to Latinity, without

really knowing why. It is the story of two young friends, Nisus and Euryale, who derive from their friendship, which is perhaps too passionate, the desire to accomplish military exploits. And Nisus would like to have an explanation for this love he feels for Euryale. Does it come from heaven? Does it come out of the abyss? (Is it Bergson? Or must we listen to Freud?)

Di ne hunc ardorem mentibus addunt?
Is it the gods who have given our spirits this passion?
An sua quaeque Deus fit dira cupido?
Or rather, has each made a god of his desire?

I think that God wanted mystical love and that God could want only love. If God is love and total love, he could only want to be loved or to love, to love in loving or in being loved. To prepare this love for all eternity, God made sexuality. And as a consequence, sexuality is a dividing of beings into two complementary halves that fosters the awakening of a flame within them capable of bringing together in God two individuals capable of an eternal, reciprocal love.

The sexual ecstasy that exists on the physical level should be a preparation for the eternal ecstasy it symbolizes. Just as all ecstasy is fruitful in itself, so also is sexual ecstasy, and superabundantly so. "Action is never but an enfeeblement of contemplation" (Plotinus). The sexuality of which I am speaking here extends well beyond its genetic content. It is not certain organs, but the whole body that is sexual in so far as it is incomplete, unachieved, sex being the means by which it desires to become other through another. And in this sense, the feminine organism is more sexual than the masculine organism.

Physical and spiritual beings at the same time, we must serve as a channel and as a filter for all that is flesh in us in order to take it into a higher, sublime existence. Without doubt, this is one way of understanding our destiny here below. The forms of sublimation are multiple and it would be a great mistake to see them only in the realm of love. The sublimation of which we are speaking here goes beyond this; it extends to all aspects of physical life. The word sexuality focuses attention on a much too limited point, not to mention the fact that it has been corrupted in common usage. Beside this localized sexuality, a diffuse sensibility exists that is undoubtedly linked to the still-misunderstood stimulation of hormones and that comes to color the use of the other senses. It gives them a special vibration, a phosphorescence, an effervescence, and it is the reason for the secret relationship between sexuality and beauty that musicians and painters cannot ignore. At puberty, or at the time of love's awakening, colors and sounds, the excitement of the countryside, the impressions of art, all have more intensity. Deep within the other senses, there is at play, like a more delicate touch, some vital sense that it would be wrong to call sexual, but that nevertheless derives from sexual existence. Where can the first awakening of this sense be found? It is undoubtedly linked to moistness, to the warmth of the maternal womb, to the well-being of fire and hearth, to the freshness of water, of air, of things that envelop and lightly touch, to these primitive elements that the romantics have sung and Bachelard has rediscovered. Newborn love awakens these prehistoric emotions, these quests for cave, nest, intimacy, this manger where the child was born under the breath of beasts.

Nerve organs develop in two ways. In the centers, the nerve mass undergoes an increase in volume but remains

undifferentiated and homogeneous. In the peripheral organs, on the other hand, particularly in the sense organs, the
nerve threads become extremely fine, so that the brain
appears to be an organ capable of drawing more and more
profound meaning from more and more delicate stimulations. One might wonder if the erotic impression does not
have an analogous finality for the psychic being—I mean, if
nature does not intend to make the stimulations of the
genetic sense finer and finer while at the same time it makes
them capable, through the work of the brain, of serving as a
stimulant and hormone to a great number of other psychic
properties. It would be the same for man as for the animal,
whom castration deprives not only of its ability to repro-
duce but also of its energy, its savage strength. In the lover,
a new phosphorescence can be seen in the exercise of his
whole body and all his thoughts. Each of the other senses—
sight, hearing, the perception of forms and volumes—all of
them are stimulated. *Sexus intus alit et magno se corpore miscet.*
It is a kind of natural magic. The time of life when these
stimulations begin to be felt in body and spirit is called
puberty. It is significant that this is also the moment when
originality, personality and even heroism are awakened.

The perspectives that I have just discussed also lend some
clarity to the mystery of original sin.

ASCETICISM AS A CORRECTIVE
FOR EROS INVERTED BY ORIGINAL SIN

If, in God's original plan, the sexual ecstasy of Adam and
Eve was really intended to help them proceed to mystical
love, it is certain that the sin they committed inverted

Eros—that *Eros*, instead of being the means for union with God, became, on the contrary, a means of egoistic self-gratification, of enjoyment turned in toward self, of cruelty and of all the inversions and perversions of lust.

So that in our time and condition, the sublimation of *Eros* demands two actions: a negative action in which it is necessary to kill the sin in ourselves, a hard action that can never be omitted from any spirituality. Over the centuries, it is Christian asceticism that has been uniquely stressed and rightly so. But there exists another action that has not yet been stressed—one left to the next millennium to develop (a millennium which will perhaps be shortened by the acceleration of time). This is not at all an act of negation, but rather one of transference, of *sublimation*—an action by which we take *Eros* and sublimate it in trying as much as possible, not to repress it, but to use it for the purpose of divine union.

And this is what explains the fact that, in our sinful state, there have been two ways of approaching God—two ways that are necessarily separate and that cannot be united—the way of virginity and the way of marriage.

VIRGINITY

Here it is necessary to understand that virginity is not the negation of *Eros*, but, on the contrary, a state in which, by isolation, vow, discipline and meditation, the virgin, the vowed one (be it man or woman) must not destroy a fundamental energy, but, rather, concentrate it on God! And how? By mortification.

It must be understood that all forms of mortification—whether it be mortification in regard to money (poverty), autonomy (obedience), sex (chastity) or any of the other mortifications which some among the great mystics practiced nearly to the point of death (e.g., mortification of the digestion or of breathing)—are for the purpose, not of annihilating, but, on the contrary, of vivifying and of preparing for the resurrection of the body.

I picture this to myself in the form of a bow. The one who mortifies himself bends a bow, he stretches a cord—he goes in a direction contrary to life. For example, he mortifies autonomy in himself; he is obedient. He mortifies his desire for money; he is poor. He mortifies his sexuality; he is chaste. He seems to renounce. In reality, he sets the arrow. And the more he mortifies himself, the more quickly and strongly the arrow will fly. Thus, the mortification of erotic energy is not the annihilation of this energy, but a concentration of this energy. As a result, instead of turning horizontally toward procreation, this energy rises, goes vertically, purifies itself and turns toward the Creator.

One aspect of asceticism consists in taking lower-level energy and making it go from the horizontal state (where it resides with us) to the vertical, where it attains to God alone. And it is for this reason that Father Teilhard said: "Virgins are at the utmost tip of cosmic evolution." Virginity concentrates cosmic energy, it turns it toward the ultimate state; it proclaims this redemption of the cosmos, which groans, as Paul said.

MARRIAGE

There is another state of life through which we can sublimate *Eros*. It is that which Pope Pius XI called *Casti Connubii*—it is marriage, in so far as marriage is chaste.

Chastity is an energy that regulates the use of the senses; it is a form of temperance. It differs from continence which from the first renounces this use. Conjugal chastity is not abstinence, but rather wisdom, measure, melody, the art of loving. *Eros* in marriage aspires at the same time to both procreation and union—but the union is at the same time union with the other and union with God. One can love only in God, whether it be in friendship or in love. For friendship and love are exchanges made with the intention of helping the two be more and better themselves and to attain their ultimate goal, which is eternal union with the Divine Love. And this, which is true of the loftiest spiritual friendships (such as that of St. Francis de Sales and St. Chantal) is also true of virtually all friendships and all loves. Chastity, moderation, tact, delicacy, reserve, courtesy, decency intervene in all unions to prevent them from becoming inverted, dissipated, to help them endure, grow, and last forever.

The energy contained in *Eros* can attain its natural and supernatural end only if certain means are taken to mortify it of all excess, to assure a healthy sublimation. Consider the difference between what I am saying and what is usually said on the subject. Conjugal life is already, in my opinion, an initiation into divine love—and not only because it is desired by God as the means of procreation, nor even as the means of union between souls. It is an initiation into divine love for a very hidden reason—it is because the "flames of love", as the bride of the Song says, "are the flames of Yahweh". That is to say, the emotions and impulses must always be tempered by this unobtrusive force called decency, which is a part of all human and reasonable use of sex.

The chaste use of sex is not only a symbol, it is a foretaste of the resurrection of the flesh.

You will find analagous thoughts in Father Teilhard when he says that the feminine insures the transfiguration of the cosmos—or when he writes, "The feminine is Christ transposed in the Virgin."

You will also find these thoughts in Russian mysticism, for example in Merejkovski, who said, "Decency conceals sex, but sex conceals God", and who teaches that the resurrection of the flesh will only be fully understood when sexuality is considered in a new way. Here are areas which, although not inaccessible, have yet to be explored by philosophy or even by Christian mysticism.

And it is, furthermore, why I consider the encyclical *Humanae Vitae* to be so profound. It strives to preserve conjugal union from all mechanical or chemical distortion, from all "desacralization", in order to make it capable of becoming the means of a state of union with God.

It is fashionable to place the popes in opposition to each other. It is more correct to look for the continuity in their teaching. In truth, the encyclical *Humanae Vitae* extends and applies the encyclical *Casti Connubii*. Perhaps one day they will be combined into one·composite text: *Castum Humanae Connubium Vitae?*

On that day, we will understand that there is a relation between *Eros* and *Agape*, we will approach the ultimate mystery—the mystery of divine love—about which I would like to say a word. I recall another book that I wrote, on the Virgin Mary. We live in a creation dislocated by sin, where, in order to live, it is necessary to choose between two mutually exclusive paths. It is necessary to choose between virginity consecrated to God on the one hand, and, on the other, marriage, which insures fruitfulness but which, in a certain sense, diminishes the opportunities for contemplation by undertaking the concerns of everyday life. The ideal would be to have these two states interpenetrate, help, respect and revitalize each other. Consecrated persons could adopt families. Family associations could be established around centers of charity and of contemplative, sacrificial life. And the service would be mutual. If married people need the spirit of virginity, the reverse is also true—consecrated ones need to know the trials of marriage. Above all, they need to avoid holy egotism!

A mutual appreciation, a convergence could be established, then, between these two states of life. It is still clearly understood that, theoretically, the state of virginity vowed to God and to universal service, offers in principle the greater possibility of love, that it is in itself a visible holocaust. But it is the degree of invisible love that constitutes the inner value, that God alone knows.

Let me repeat that the human spirit, in order to unite in itself and in God what creation at present realizes in different and, as I just said, complementary states, would need a model—one that is both ideal and real, temporal and eternal, historical and eschatological, in whom virginity, the married state and fruitfulness would be mysteriously integrated, substantially united.

For the Christian and Catholic faith, this synthesizing, dialectical, structured individual is not an abstract myth, but a concrete, real mystery. It is the mystery of the Virgin Mother of God.

JOSEPH DE LESTAPIS, S.J.

A Summary of Karol Wojtyla's
Love and Responsibility

Karol Wojtyla was once a Marxist. His was a belated vocation: born in 1920, he entered the seminary only after having first been a worker, then a student of arts and letters and one of the collaborators of Mieczyslaw Kotlarczyk, founder of the Rhapsodic Theatre in Cracow. His work *Love and Responsibility: A Study of Sexual Morality* was published in 1961. It was the second edition of 1962 that was translated into French and appeared in 1965.[1]

It is a highly structured work, the fruit of vigorous reflection. It would be paradoxical to say that, because it draws its inspiration from recent developments in psychology and psychoanalysis, it is a refreshing change from all the recent essays on love. In fact, Wojtyla's work is difficult, even, frankly, a bit forbidding at first glance in requiring so much concentration, reflection and even logic on the part of the reader. But it is precisely by doing so that it renews us, for

[1] Karol Wojtyla, Archbishop-Metropolitan of Cracow, *Amour et responsabilité, étude de morale sexuelle*, trans. from Polish by Thérèse Sas, reviewed by Marie-Andrée Bouchaud-Kalinowska, Preface by Henri de Lubac (1965) 286 p. [Numbers in parentheses refer to this French edition. Ed.]

it turns us from the facility—perhaps even from a certain superficiality—of phenomenological analysis. The author ignores none of these disciplines. He knows how to make use of them when necessary. But what interests him is plunging, not into depth psychology, but into psychology's depths. He comes, then, necessarily to the metaphysical level of the spirit. And it is this which is both rewarding and arresting, as is the case, moreover, with all spiritual effort.

Although the undertaking is difficult, we will try to give some idea of the structure of this work and its developments. The book is comprised of four large chapters of around sixty pages, each consisting of about ten sections: 1) The Person and Sexuality; 2) The Person and Love; 3) The Person and Chastity; 4) Justice toward the Creator. An appendix—Sexology and Morality—completes the whole.

I. THE PERSON AND SEXUALITY

The objective of the first chapter is to pose the following dilemma: utilitarian axiology[2] or personalist axiology. It is in fact a question of knowing whether or not one person can use another, if one can offer himself the enjoyment of the other. This is the work's starting point. An officer uses his soldiers and the head of a business uses his employees. What is to be understood by that? Can man be a mere means by which another man achieves the goals he sets for himself? Are there not grounds for considering the same question in the relationship between man and woman?

---

[2] "Axiology" is a technical name for the science of values.

The Nature of the Person: Can a person be used?

"The term person has been chosen in order to stress that man cannot be confined in the notion 'individual of the species', that there is something more in him, a particular fullness and perfection of being, which cannot be expressed otherwise than by using the word person" (14).

"In more vivid terms we could say that the person, considered as a subject, is distinguished from even the highest order of animals, by his *interiority*, where a life that is uniquely his own is concentrated: his interior life. This cannot be said of animals, even though their organisms may be subject to similar biophysiological processes and connected with a constitution that more or less resembles that of man" (14).

Having said this, do we have the right to treat the person as a means and to use him as such?

The answer is that the person can only be the object of love. To love is the opposite of to *use*. To love is the opposite of to *enjoy*. This principle has absolutely universal implications (19). "This norm, in its negative aspect, states that the person is a good that is incompatible with utilization, that cannot be treated as an object of enjoyment, and therefore as a means. Its positive aspect is unfolded along parallel lines: the person is a good such that only love can dictate the appropriate and valid attitude in his regard" (33).

Consequently: Pleasure is not a norm

A certain number of consequences are going to follow, and among others, this one: pleasure, which is a value, is not a norm. Pleasure is not only not a norm for me in what would be indisputable egoism; but it is not even a norm when I have decided to focus my action on others. In fact, in a self-centered attitude as in an other-centered one, to take pleasure as a norm is to sink back into utilitarianism.

"Pleasure, by its very nature, is only a present good and concerns only the subject at hand; it is not a transsubjective good"[3] (30). Pleasure is not in fact the sole good; neither is it the *essential* goal of human action. In essence, it is only a peripheral, subordinate thing that can occur because of action. Consequently, "to organize action solely in view of pleasure is contrary to the structure of human acts" (28). We know in fact that many things which can fail to bring us pleasure can still be fundamentally good for us.[4] In this sense, to wish one's neighbor the "greatest pleasure" is not at all equivalent to wishing his good. There is only an appearance of altruism in that. In fact, "I appreciate the pleasure of others only through my own, because it is agreeable to see the others experience it. But if such a thing ceases to give me pleasure, or, indeed, no longer arises from my calculation of happiness (a term very often used by utilitarians), I no longer feel bound by the pleasure of others, which is no longer a good and can even become an evil." If I determine my action toward my neighbor in terms of this norm of pleasure, "I will then tend to eliminate

[3] "Transsubjective" is a neologism by which the author wishes to make us conscious not only of the objective character of the good but also its universality.

[4] The father of a family who is about to take the road in an automobile with them sacrifices the pleasure that a good meal with a bottle of fine wine would have given him, preferring instead the greater good of a truly safe trip on the road.

the pleasure of the other when no pleasure is connected with it any more for myself, or at best it will become unimportant to me and I will no longer be concerned about it" (30).

My apparent altruism reveals itself in the end to be a subtle form of egoism. I am interested in the other only in proportion as I see in him a reflection of what I am, of what I feel.

"The only solution to this inevitable egoism is to recognize, outside of purely subjective good, i.e., outside of pleasure, the objective good that can itself also unite persons as it assumes the character of common good. It is this good that is the veritable foundation of love, and the persons who choose it together yield to it at the same time. Because of that, they bind themselves with a true, objective bond of love that allows them to free themselves from subjectivism and from the inevitable egoism that proceeds from it. Love is communion of persons" (30).

Characteristics of Human Sexuality:
1) It is a tendency

Having set forth these principles, the author then introduces sexuality as an *admitted* fact essential to human relations. The first question he asks himself is whether sexuality is instinct or impulse. If by instinct is understood "a spontaneous manner of acting, not subject to reflection", he says, this way of acting is typical of animal behavior; it is not typical of man who possesses precisely the faculty of reflecting upon the relationship of the means to the end. "By his nature man is capable of action that rises above the instinctive level." He is capable of this in the sexual domain as in all others. It is better, consequently, to speak of sexual impulse or tendency, as a natural and congenital orientation according to which man develops, but which he owes it to himself to assume consciously and with reflection.

2) An "other-centered" tendency

The author next distinguishes very clearly between the sexual tendency and the tendency toward preservation.[5] "The tendency toward preservation serves, as its name indicates, to preserve, to safeguard the existence of the given being, man or animal. . . . To characterize it, we could say that it is *egocentric* to the extent that by its nature it is centered in the existence of one's self, considered as such. Hence, the tendency toward preservation differs essentially from the sexual tendency. In fact, the natural orientation of this latter always transcends the self; its immediate object is another being of the opposite sex and of the same species and its ultimate end is the existence of the species. Unlike the tendency toward preservation, there is something that could be called 'other-centeredness'. This is precisely what constitutes the foundation of love" (57–58).

3) An existential tendency

Is the sexual tendency an accidental or an existential one? In other words, is its only goal to perfect someone in a more or less contingent way, or does it rather have, among other

[5] Which urges man to feed himself, to sleep, etc.

goals, that of "purely and simply causing someone to exist"? It is necessary to reply to this question that "it is precisely this relation to the existence of man and that of the species *homo* that gives the sexual impulse its objective importance and significance" (45).

But existence does not constitute the proper and adequate object of any natural science. Existence itself is the object of philosophy which alone applies itself to the problem of existence as such. Hence the gravity and seriousness with which the sexual tendency must be considered and discussed. If the latter "had only a *biological* significance, it could be considered as one kind of enjoyment; it could be acknowledged that it constitutes an object of enjoyment for man to the same degree as for various other natural living or inanimate beings. But since it possesses this existential character, since it is connected to the very existence of the human person, to the foremost and fundamental good of the latter, the sexual tendency must be subject to the principles that bind the whole person. Thus, even though the (sexual) impulse may be at man's disposition, he must never make use of it without love toward a person, nor, what would be still worse, use it against that love" (44).

Two False Explanations of Sexuality

Logic would thus require us to dismiss two explanations of the sexual tendency for the reason that neither takes the personalist norm into real consideration. On the one hand, explaining the sexual tendency in terms of the libido entails an egocentric conception. This explanation leads straight to utilitarianism and cannot, therefore, be admitted.

Another explanation, although apparently just the opposite, fails by the same kind of reasoning: the sexual tendency is only a means conceived by nature to gain control over the human person and subordinate him to procreation. There also, in opposition to a personalist axiology, we sink once again into a utilitarian axiology where the communion of persons as such is not taken into consideration. As "strict" as this conception of sexuality appears, it is nonetheless disastrous for the development of the person and of love, as is, moreover, the "libidinous" conception.

II. THE PERSON AND LOVE

The second chapter proceeds to a threefold analysis of love: metaphysical, psychological and moral.

The Metaphysical Components of Love

From the metaphysical point of view, love is expressed by the *attraction* (the *amor concupiscentiae* of medieval philosophy) which is a reaction to some particular value present in a person. The attraction in turn reveals a lack to be filled in the subject and expresses his *desire* for the other as for a good for himself (*amor complacentiae*). From this point of view, "love comes as close as possible to utility while permeating it with its own essence. Nevertheless, a true love of concupiscence is never transformed into a utilitarian attitude for it always (even in sensual desire) has its roots in the personalist principle" (73).

Finally, love of concupiscence does not exhaust the essence of love between persons. "When a man desires someone as a good for himself, it is necessary for him to want the person desired truly to be a good, so that she can really be a good for the one who desires her. It is in this way that the connection between concupiscence and *benevolence* becomes evident" (74).[6] Such an analysis of love could lead us to forget that the love of the man and of the woman is not only a reality of one for the other, that it is not only in the man and in the woman—for then it would be fundamentally two loves. But love is one, something that exists *between them*. Hence love's new metaphysical character of being a reciprocity between persons. "A reciprocal love forms the most immediate foundation from which a single 'we' is born of two 'I's'. It is in this that its natural dynamism consists" (77).

Love Is "Gratuitous Reciprocity"

"True reciprocity cannot be born of two egoisms."

"If what the two persons bring into love is solely or principally concupiscence seeking enjoyment and pleasure, then the reciprocity itself will be devoid of the characteristics of which we have just spoken. One person cannot trust another if he knows the other is only aiming toward enjoyment and pleasure. Neither can he trust if he himself acts in this way. This is the reverse of that characteristic of love by which it creates an interpersonal community. All that is necessary is for one of the persons to adopt a utilitarian attitude and the problem of love's reciprocity soon arises, attended by suspicions and jealousies. . . . The man and the

---

[6] Attraction and desire are egocentric. Benevolence and sympathy are gratuitous and altruistic.

woman can be a source of sexual pleasure and of various benefits for each other, but neither the pleasure alone nor sexual delight is a good which unites and binds the persons with any permanence, as Aristotle very rightly said" (78–79).

Psychological Components of Love

Such considerations lead us to a further analysis of love, this time as a psychological reality. The author begins this by studying love's elemental components: *perception* and the *emotion* that proceeds from it. "We call perception," he says, "the reaction of the senses to the stimuli produced by objects. . . . Man has a great number of perceptions. The sensory receptors are continuously at work. . . . Some perceptions are lasting and strong, others weak and transitory. Sensory perception is often associated with a certain emotion" (92–93).

Emotion is a different phenomenon from perception: in emotion we experience one of the values of the object. When perception is united to emotion, their object penetrates man's consciousness and takes form in it with all the more clarity. Emotion allows two persons, the man and the woman, to experience each other reciprocally as values. Two large categories of values are then presented, the values of sensuality and those of affectivity.

1) Sensuality

Sensuality perceives the sexual values of the body of the person of the opposite sex. This orientation of sexuality is spontaneous and instinctive, and as such it is not morally bad but quite natural. But "the orientation toward the sexual values of the body as the object of enjoyment requires integration. It must find its place within a valid attitude with regard to the person, without which it would not be love" (97–98).

The idea of "sex appeal", to the extent that it presents these values as independent or sufficient in themselves and consequently cuts off the path to their integration into a personal and complete love, is a dead-end, not to say a contradiction or a perversion—another manifestation of the utilitarian axiology.

2) Affectivity

It is necessary to make a clear distinction between affectivity and sensuality. . . . Sensuality retains in its perception of the other only the body dissociated from everything else. By contrast, affectivity (like perception) reacts to the person as a whole. The sexual values perceived remain attached to the entire person and are not limited to his body. That is why this sensual orientation does not stand out in affectivity. The latter is not a "consumer". This is why it can include contemplative moments related to the beautiful, to the perception of aesthetic values, for example. "The affectivity of man is permeated with admiration for femininity, that of woman with admiration for masculinity, but within these limits no desire for enjoyment even appears" (101).

Affectivity is fruitful in the sense that man desires that various values be found in the person who is the object of his love; affection, aided by the imagination, creates them and endows her with them so that the affective bond will be the more complete. Thus, "under the influence of affectivity, the value of the object concerned often grows inordinately.

Affective love remains under the influence of the imagination" (102–103). This is the principal source of the weakness of affective love. It is often in danger of lacking realism. Like sensuality, it must also be integrated into love. Affection, which suffers from subjectivity, must acquire its truth by being integrated with love, which aims at authenticity. Love in fact requires an objective *truth*, for which *freedom* is a necessary condition.

Moral Analysis of Love

Such requirements now demand a moral analysis of love. Since love is a matter of truth and freedom, of truth in the understanding and of freedom in the will, we are in the domain of morality. It is now the moment, therefore, to examine love between man and woman as *virtue*.

Love as virtue has "the value (of the other) as person" in view. The value of the person is bound up with his entire being and not just with his sex, which is only one characteristic of his being. This value of the person is not the object of sensual or sensible perception but of intellectual and conceptual knowledge and of free, voluntary consent. "It is the will that is the source of this affirmation of the person's value" (113). Love as virtue "is formed in the will and utilizes its resources of spiritual potentiality, that is, it constitutes a real engagement of the freedom of the personal subject founded on the truth concerning the personal object" (113).

Love: Voluntary gift in view of a communion in the good

Since it is a voluntary gift, love is completely different from the mere carnal surrender of the woman to the man.

Love is essentially, on both sides, the will to belong to the other. The virtue of love can only be "sponsal".[7] "It is reciprocity and friendship founded on a communion in the good" (116). It is this common will to attain the good and to confer it on each other mutually that manifests the objective aspect of love. It is in fact in this "objective aspect" that authentic love is recognized.

While affectivity "is characterized by an idealization of its object, love that is concentrated on the value of the person makes us love the latter as he really is: not the idea that we have formed of him, but the real individual. We love him with his virtues and his faults, and, up to a certain point, independently of his virtues and despite his faults. The measure of such a love appears most clearly at the moment when its object makes a mistake, when his weaknesses and even his sins become evident. The man who truly loves not only does not withhold his love at that time, but on the contrary, while being aware of the faults and deficiencies and without approving of them, loves still more. For the person himself never loses his essential value as person. An affection that attends to the value of the person remains faithful to man" (123–24).

Such are the characteristics of the virtue of love: a will to truth, the chosen person tends to be apprehended in all his truth; a will toward gift and total belonging to the other in terms of the good that is wished him, or more exactly, the good that is necessary for him. "Love of the will (love as virtue) is especially expressed in the desire of good for the person loved. . . . Thus by benefiting from the natural dynamism of the will, true love does its best to introduce into the relations between man and woman a note of fundamental unselfishness, so as to liberate their love from the

[7] The adjective "sponsal" is derived from *sponsus, sponsa*: spouse.

attitude of (utilitarian) enjoyment. . . . The (sexual or affective) tendency wants above all to take, to make use of another person; love, by contrast, wants to give, to create good, to make happy. . . . The great moral strength of true love lies precisely in this desire for the true good of another person" (125–27).

Far from being a thunderbolt, love is rather a free creation. This is why it belongs to the domain of morality. If its immediate norm is the "value of the person", its ultimate norm is the relationship for which this person exists.

III. THE PERSON AND CHASTITY

The preceding analyses have shown that love "cannot reside only in a subjective state, where the energies of sexuality and affectivity aroused by the sexual tendency are manifested, for it would not then reach its personal level nor would it unite persons" (135). Love in fact can unite persons only in terms of the good they appreciate, seek and pursue in common, in each other and for each other. The wills are thus united because they desire the same good as their goal; emotions merge because they experience in common the same values.

It has been said that affective exuberance and the violence of sexual desire "confer on love its flavor, but do not supply its objective essence" (135). In order for true love (the virtue, love) to assert itself upon these two often tumultuous attendants and make them consent to being integrated, i.e., consent to serve the values of the person and not eclipse them nor relegate them to the background, a "virtue" is necessary: chastity.

Just as the failure to integrate sensuality and affectivity indicates a moral underdevelopment of love, of which eroticism, moreover, is the surest sign, so also a successful integration of *Eros* and *Philia* (we are using this word to designate affectivity and tenderness) denotes a rich development of the virtue of love. Chastity is the sign, and even more than the sign, of this development: its diligence brings it about. Chastity is the humble *deus ex machina* of this so desirable integration.

Rehabilitation of Chastity

"Max Scheler found that it was necessary to rehabilitate virtue (chastity among others) because he had discerned in contemporary man a spiritual attitude inconsistent with its true value, an attitude he called "resentment".[8] Resentment consists in a false attitude with regard to values.

The virtue of chastity will be rehabilitated in this way only to the extent that we perfectly understand its function, which is, as we have just said, to restore the concupiscence of sensuality and the subjectivity of affectivity to their proper place in moral love.

We know that concupiscence is a reaction to the body as the possible object of enjoyment. Concupiscence seeks its

---

[8] "Resentment is a lack of objectivity in judgment and appreciation, having its source in the weakness of the will. In fact, to attain or realize a higher value, we must make a greater effort of will. Thus, to free himself subjectively from the obligation to make this effort, to convince himself of the nonexistence of this value, man reduces its importance, he refuses it the respect to which it in reality has a right, he goes so far as to see evil in it however much objectivity obliges him to see good in it. . . . An inclination toward resentment sleeps within the soul of all men" (133–34).

satisfaction in the body and sex through enjoyment. It only serves to direct the psychological dynamism of the subject toward these values by arousing an "interest" in them. It unfortunately risks becoming absorbed in them, drowning in them. It is the duty of chastity to "restrain" this concupiscence within its proper proportions, in that way preventing a detrimental waste of the "materials" destined for the virtue of love.

Along with concupiscence, affectivity, which is the faculty of reacting to sexual values connected with the person of the opposite sex and not to the values of the body as the possible object of enjoyment, can equally be the occasion of "absorption" and "drowning" in a subjectivity of sentiment.

"The feelings play a very important role in the formation of the subjective aspect of love, which does not exist without affection" (142), but the subjectivity of feelings, by bringing about even a subjectivity of values, is equivalent to an orientation toward the subtle pleasure of one's own affective needs. *Egoism of the sentiment is in fact a seeking of self rather than a seeking of pleasure.*

Here again, it is for chastity to restore affectivity to its subordinate place within the scope of virtuous love. Since egoism of the sentiment is as disastrous an impairment of love as egoism of the senses, and since chastity is the virtue whose role is to integrate sensuality and affectivity within the virtue of love, it follows that there cannot be authentic love without the positive action of chastity.

Sinful Love

"Sinful love is nothing other than a form of man-woman relationship in which feeling, and particularly pleasure, has grown to the point of assuming the proportions of an autonomous good, deciding everything without taking into account the *objective value of the person*—neither the laws nor the objective principles of coexistence and relations between persons of different sex" (154).

It has already been stated that sensuality and concupiscence of the body are natural reactions to the sexual values present in the other. Consequently, neither "sensuality nor even concupiscence of the body are sinful in themselves, for only a voluntary act, conscious and consented to, can be sinful. . . . It is only at the moment when the will consents, when it begins to want what is happening in the realm of sensuality and to agree to carnal desire that man himself begins to act, at first interiorly—the will being the immediate source of internal acts—then exteriorly. These acts then possess a moral value, are good or bad, and in the latter case are called sins" (149–50).

The will's mastery *over itself*, however, is not the same thing as the indirect mastery it can have over sensuality. "No one can in fact demand of himself that the reactions of sensuality not manifest themselves in him nor that they subside as soon as the will refuses to consent to them. This is important for the practice of the virtue of continence. 'Not to want' is different from 'not to feel', 'not to experience' " (150–51).

Just as sin is born of the failure to subordinate sensuality to the value of the person, so also can it be born of a failure to subordinate affectivity. The latter gives rise to what was previously called *subjectivity of the sentiment*, which in turn provokes the *subjectivity of values* by which, contrary to the perception of good by the conscience, what is agreeable is deemed good. This "makes one believe incorrectly that the subjective state of affective saturation is already a valid love, that this state is the whole of love. . . . The particular danger of 'sinful love' resides in a fiction, namely in the fact that it is experienced in its first moments and before any reflection, not as 'sinful' but chiefly as 'love'. It is true that this circumstance diminishes, directly, the gravity of the sin, but indirectly it increases the danger" (153). The *"subjectivization" of love takes place without the knowledge of the subject*, who is in danger of establishing himself in a fictitious situation, causing him to turn his back on the true common good of the persons concerned and of their will to communion.

Return to Chastity: Its true nature

The greater and richer the chastity possessed by the subject concerned, the less frequent and probable will be the deviations described above, brought about by the non-integration of sensuality and affectivity into true love. "This virtue of chastity is in fact nothing but the aptitude to master the movements of concupiscence. Aptitude means more than capacity. Virtue is a 'permanent' aptitude; if it were transitory, it would not be virtue. One could say, if it were not permanent, that one was *fortunate* to master a movement of concupiscence, whereas virtue guarantees such behavior" (157).

It is again appropriate to stress the true nature of chastity for "very often chastity is understood to be like a blind restraint of sensuality and carnal impulses which pushes the values of the body and sex back into the subconscious where they simply wait for an opportunity to explode. . . . Because of this idea (which is false), the virtue of chastity is often thought to have a purely negative character, to be only a series of 'noes'. On the contrary, it is first of all a 'yes', from which the 'noes' then follow" (158). It is a yes to the value of the person. "The essence of chastity consists in not 'falling behind' the value of the person and in raising to its level all reaction to the values of the body and sex. This requires a considerable interior and spiritual effort, for affirmation of the person can only be the fruit of the spirit. Far from being negative and destructive, this effort is positive and creative 'from within' " (159).[9]

It would thus be desirable in the future to substitute, in public opinion, for the wholly negative idea of a "castrating" chastity, the wholly positive idea of an operational mastery, of a permanent aptitude for achieving the integration of the more or less blind forces of sensuality and affectivity within the virtue of love, a love that is the common will for good.

An Excursus on Modesty

It is rather easy to describe the apparent characteristics of modesty. It is much more difficult to give the metaphysical and personalist sense of this behavior.

"Modesty is the tendency, totally unique to the human being, to conceal his sexual values to the extent that they would be liable to obscure the value of the person. It is a defensive movement of the person who does not wish to be an object of enjoyment, either in act or in intention, but

[9] Unfortunately, and we need only ask around us to be convinced of it, the great majority of people identify chastity with abstinence, when chastity is actually much more.

who wishes, on the contrary, to be the object of love. Capable of becoming an object of enjoyment precisely because of his sexual gifts, the person seeks to hide them. He hides them, however, only in part for, wishing to remain an object of love, he must allow them to be perceptible to the extent that love needs them to be awakened and to live. On a par with this form of modesty (which could be called 'modesty of the body', for sexual gifts are externally related with the body particularly) is another form, which we have called 'modesty of the acts of love' and which is a tendency to conceal the reactions which manifest the attitude of enjoyment regarding the body and sex. This tendency derives from the fact that the body and sex belong to the person, who cannot be an object of enjoyment. Only love is capable of truly absorbing both forms of modesty" (174).

Conversely, immodesty (which is called pornography in art) "is a tendency in the (presentation or) representation of the human body and of love to place the accent on sex in order to bring about in the reader or spectator the conviction that sexual values are the only object of love, being the only values of the person. This tendency is harmful for it is destructive of the integral image of love previously described" (179). Modesty that contains an element of shame, whose immediate effect is to conceal sexual qualities, lasts as long as love is growing and, in the meantime, is transformed. In fact, "the feeling of love has the power to absorb that of shame, to free the subject's consciousness of shame. . . . The latter disappears when the conviction is born that the sexual qualities theretofore concealed no longer arouse only 'sexual desire', and that concupiscence is accompanied by an affective attitude" (172).

Chastity Is Exercised by Continence

To effect this integration of the values of the body and sex into love, which is itself completely centered in the value of the person, chastity ordinarily calls forth a certain behavior: continence. "This term suggests that the principal method has something in common with the action of containing" (182).

Continence can in fact be defined as "an aptitude for controlling the concupiscence of the body by the will and for moderating the sensual reactions of affectivity" (183).

Continence, however, is not in itself a virtue. Blind continence is not enough. "There can be no genuine continence unless the objective order of values is recognized: the value of the person is above the values of sex. . . . And even more, it is only as this value of the person progressively takes possession of the consciousness and the will that one becomes calm and frees himself from the characteristic feeling of frustration. It is well known that the practice of temperance and of the virtue of chastity is accompanied, especially in its first stages, by a feeling of frustration, of having renounced a value. . . . As true love of the person develops, this reflex becomes weaker, for the values reassume their proper place" (184–85).

Continence, Affectivity and Tenderness

In this process of integration, an important role has devolved upon the sublimation of feelings. Affectivity, which is "much more a desire for the presence of a human being of the opposite sex" than a desire for enjoyment, can easily support the concept of the person. "So that the spontaneous process of emotional idealization develops, not around femininity-virility values, but around the value of the person, reaching the spiritual plane through reflection. Thus the virtue of chastity and its auxiliary, continence, find a support in affectivity. This faculty of transforming enemies into allies is perhaps more characteristic of the essence of temperance and the virtue of chastity than of pure continence" (186). "This is because affectivity, we repeat, is oriented toward the person and not toward the body and sex. It is not a question of enjoying but of *feeling close*" (189).

When this feeling develops, it is even appropriate to speak much more of tenderness than of affectivity. "We feel tenderness toward a person (or even toward a nonrational being, for example, an animal or plant) when we become aware in a certain way of the bonds that unite it to us" (187). This tendency is more than sympathy. It is what Americans call 'empathy', that is, a sensitivity to the states of another's soul. Tenderness is born of the understanding of another's state of soul and tends to communicate to him how close one is to him. Tenderness is shown exteriorly by various actions that reflect it: the gesture of pressing someone against oneself, of embracing him or simply of taking his arm; these various manifestations of tenderness all have the same goal and one common interior significance: that of bonds that unite.

"Tenderness must be surrounded by a certain vigilance: it is necessary to take care that these various manifestations do not assume another significance and do not become the means of satisfying sensuality and sexual needs. . . . *Tenderness improves in quality if it is accompanied by firmness and intransigence.* A tenderness that is too facile and, especially, sentimentality do not inspire confidence. On the contrary, they arouse the suspicion that the person is seeking in his tender manifestations a means of satisfying his own affectivity and even his sensuality and his desire for enjoyment" (189–90).

Tenderness is the art of "being conscious of the entire man, of his whole person, of all the movements of his soul, however hidden, in thinking always of his true good."

"It is this tenderness that the woman expects from the man. She has a special right to it in marriage where she gives herself to the man, where she endures such difficult and important moments and periods in her life as pregnancy, childbearing and all that is connected with it. Her affective life is generally richer than a man's, and consequently her need for tenderness is greater. The man also needs it but not to the same degree and in another form" (193).

Finally, let us again stress that "there cannot be true tenderness without the true continence derived from a will always ready to love and triumph over the attitude of enjoyment which sensuality and concupiscence try to impose. Without continence and chastity, the natural energies of sensuality and those of affectivity that are drawn into their orbit would become only 'material' for the egoism of the senses, and eventually for that of the sentiments. . . . In contrast, it is continence that liberates from this attitude and from this egoism and, in so doing, indirectly fashions love" (193–94).

IV. THE PERSON AND JUSTICE

The idea that unites all that has been advanced in the preceding pages is this: "The person is a good to which love alone constitutes the appropriate and valid attitude"(33). This could be expressed by saying that the "personalist norm" is the commandment of love.

"In observing that the person cannot be the object of enjoyment but only an object of love, the personalist norm indicates that to which the person has a right as a person. Thus love presupposes justice" (231). "We can say that justice demands that the person be loved, and that it would be contrary to justice to use the person as a means" (34).

When the virtue of justice is called forth, the idea of "order" appears immediately. "Justice is indispensable in the order of the coexistence of persons and for their common life" (231). In this sense, it is justice that gives rise to marriage. "Marriage, in fact, as an institution, is indispensable for *justifying* the fact of the sexual relations of man and woman, especially in their own eyes and at the same time in the eyes of society" (209). "Love needs this recognition and this justification without which it is not complete. The difference in meaning attributed to words such as 'mistress', 'concubine', 'kept woman', etc. and to 'spouse' or 'fiancée' is not due to pure convention" (207). The difference is recognized in fact, because outside of marriage, sexual relations ipso facto place the person in the position of being an object of enjoyment. The contrary occurs when sexual relations between man and woman are ordered above all to integration into love. They then ask society for official recognition.

"By marriage, the man and woman become, in some way, the property of one another. This explains the need to justify it, on the one hand, to themselves and, on the other, before the Creator" (210).

The justice of man and woman toward the Creator comprises two elements: obeying the order of nature and safeguarding the value of the person. These two elements are inseparable.

The order of coexistence among persons has its foundation in the order of nature. In fact, "since he is a creature, since he depends on God for his existence, and, just like other creatures, owes God his nature, man must use his reason to discern the laws of the Creator that have found their expression in the objective order of nature and then to formulate human laws in harmony with them. . . . Only then will man be just in relation to the Creator" (233).

But at the same time, "Man and woman will not discharge their duty of justice toward the Creator by the sole act of reproduction (the objective of the order of nature). The person exceeds nature, and the order of persons goes beyond that of nature. This is why conjugal relations satisfy the justice due to the Creator only when they are placed on the level of love, i.e., of a true union of two persons" (234).

Justice and Indissoluble Monogamy

By using his reason, as has just been said, man will discover that "it is just" for marriage to be monogamous and indissoluble. "Temptations to find a solution to the problem of marriage outside of strict monogamy (which implies indissolubility) are contrary to the personalist norm and do not correspond to its requirements because they admit that one person can be an object of enjoyment for another, a danger that especially threatens the woman. This is so in the two instances of polygamy: polygyny and polyandry" (197). If a man has possessed a woman as his spouse, by a legal marriage, and if, after a certain time, he leaves her to marry another, he proves by so doing that his spouse represented only sexual values for him. In the light of these principles, i.e., the personalist norm, "it must be granted that in the case where the common life of the husband and wife becomes impossible, for really serious reasons . . . only one possibility of separation exists: separation of the spouses without dissolution of the marriage" (201).

If these truths are difficult to recognize, it is because reflection has not yet managed to raise itself to the level of the virtue of love, of love in the integrally objective sense. It has remained at the level where love is only taken in the psychological and subjective sense of the word.

Love, Justice and Procreation

Let us repeat one more time that "in the order of love, man can remain faithful to the person only to the degree to which he remains faithful to nature. By violating the laws of nature, he is equally violating the person by making him the object of enjoyment instead of an object of love" (217).

But, "in the conjugal relations of man and woman, two orders meet: that of nature whose end is reproduction, and the order of persons which is expressed in their love and tends toward its most complete realization. These two orders are inseparable for one depends on the other; the attitude regarding procreation is the condition for the realization of love" (213). In the world of creatures inferior to man, creatures deprived of reason, the order of nature is realized in an instinctive way, with the participation, at the most, of sensory knowledge. In the world of men, the order of nature must be realized in a different fashion—it must be apprehended, recognized by the reason, understood. And it is only in this way, by this understanding and recognition of the order of nature, that justice is rendered to the Creator. "Man is just with regard to God when he recognizes the order of nature and respects it." "By knowing about it through his reason and by conforming his actions to it, he participates in the mind of God and takes part in the law God has given to the world in creating it" (232).

This opinion is quite the opposite of ideologies in which man's whole value derives from the fact that he is his own legislator, the source of all law and all justice (Kant). These ideologies are false; man could be his own legislator only if he were not a creature, if he were himself his first cause. He is therefore obliged to realize his freedom as a human person within the framework pre-established by the order of nature. According to this order, man has at his sovereign disposal all nonpersonal beings; he can make them the object of his use and his enjoyment. The nature of the personal being alone escapes him in the sense that he cannot arbitrarily make of it what he wishes, cannot use it as a tool or enjoy it as an object.

The question must then be posed: According to the order of nature, what is the sexual relationship between man and woman? To this question, reason responds: "With the man, conjugal relations are always tied to procreation, with the woman, they are connected to it periodically" (269). In sexual relations, the man always serves procreation by furnishing seeds of life in an overabundance. The nature of woman, on the contrary, fixes the number of possible conceptions in a precise and, one could say, "economical" way:

"in the course of the menstrual cycle, only a single ovum normally appears, the object of possible fertilization, and this is independent of the frequency of relations (with the exception of certain pathological cases). . . . It is thus the organism of the woman that determines the number of possible children. Fertilization can take place only at the moment when her organism permits it, that is, when it has prepared for it by a series of biochemical reactions" (269–70).

Such is the "order of nature" presented by the personal constitution of man and woman. Such is the frame of reference within which the freedom of the human person can move. "Since man is a rational being, his tendency to extend the participation of his consciousness to all areas of his activity is consistent with his nature. It is the same with the tendency toward conscious maternity and paternity. The man and woman having conjugal relations should know at what moment and how they can have a child. In fact, they are responsible for each conception—responsible to themselves and before the family they are thus creating or increasing" (268).

Whereas with contraceptive techniques, "sterility is imposed against nature, in periodic continence it is caused by the natural operation of the laws of fertility" (227).

Objections to Periodic Continence

Two objections are generally raised to the use of periodic continence:

1) "It is said that to adopt such an attitude is equivalent to subordinating man to nature at a time when in so many

fields he has triumphed over it and rules it." This is only a specious argument "for man masters nature only by complying with its immanent dynamism. One does not conquer nature by violating its laws. Nature only allows domination through a profound knowledge of its finality and of the laws that govern it. Man makes use of nature by better and better utilizing its latent possibilities" (216). In other words, it is in submitting to the laws of order in nature engraved in his person that man has the best opportunity to act in a personalist way. This is subject, however, to one condition—and it is the second objection that will give the opportunity to clarify this condition—namely, that such control be governed by love and not utilitarianism.

2) "Why should periodic continence be better than artificial techniques since the one just as well as the others tends toward the same end: to eliminate procreation from conjugal relations?" (227)

"To respond to this question, it is first of all necessary to clear away many of the associations linked to the word 'method'. In speaking of the natural method, people often (incorrectly) adopt the same point of view as for 'artificial methods', i.e., that it implies utilitarian principles. Thus conceived, the natural method would no longer be anything but one of the means serving to assure the *maximum* of pleasure, except that it would achieve it by other than artificial methods. Herein lies the fundamental error. It is evident, in fact, that the method called natural is morally good only when it is correctly interpreted and applied" (227).

Now it will only be so if continence is "virtue", and like all virtue, is unselfish, concentrated on the good and not on usefulness. Without that, it would have no place in the true love of persons. Continence, which would be reduced to being only a method in the utilitarian sense of the word, could be justly considered as a contraceptive means, even if, materially, it respects the order of nature of the human person.

Continence as virtue, on the contrary, cannot be considered as a contraceptive means. In fact, as virtue, continence works in the name of chastity and for chastity, which is to say, in view of realizing the best possible integration of sensuality and affectivity into love. The sexual relations of man and woman in marriage have the full value of a union of persons only when they assume an acceptance of the possibility of procreation, such, at least, as the very nature of their sexuality presents it. This results from the synthesis of the two orders: of nature and of the person.

In fact, in their conjugal relations, man and woman are not in a relationship limited to themselves alone: owing to the force of circumstances,[10] their relations virtually embrace at certain moments the new person who, owing to their union, can be procreated. When the conjugal relations of two persons can give life to a new person, as a function of that order of nature within the framework of which human freedom is exercised, the personalist norm cannot accomodate any effective rejection, refusal or compromise whatever of this possibility.

In fact, when at this moment the man and woman *absolutely* reject this idea that "I could be a father, I could be a mother", artificially excluding it by techniques and inter-

[10] Or better, by the order of nature, foundation of the order of values of the person (cf. 213–14; 216–19; 232–34).

ventions inhibitory to their life force, far from subordinating sexual values to the value of the person, they are doing just the opposite. No longer using the sexual tendency in accord with its natural finality, they are by that very fact cutting themselves off from a true integration of their natural sexuality in their personal love.

Conclusion

To discuss love and responsibility while including sexuality and affectivity is to go far beyond the purely medical point of view.

In fact, "the medical point of view (it is necessary to take care of health and avoid illness) is only marginally connected to sexual morality where the personalist point of view (the point of view of love and responsibility) predominates." According to this point of view, "it is a matter of knowing what the man owes the woman, and vice versa, as a result of the fact that they are both persons, and not only of specifying what is beneficial to their health" (250).

"Obviously the concern for biological life and health as goods of the person enter equally into this norm that does not allow the person to be treated as an object of enjoyment and that demands that his true good be sought. But health is not his only nor his supreme good" (250).

Consequently, in seeking to resolve the problem of regulating fertility in a couple, it is not enough to adopt a merely medical or psychological point of view. "One cannot fail to take into account the essential fact that the man and the woman are persons" (219). "And if we do not wish to abandon this basis of justice and the personalist norm, we must affirm that the only 'method' of regulating births is periodic continence'' (226), the virtue of continence. For, "the virtuous practice of continence is the only solution worthy of persons that can be given to the problem of birth control'' (219).